ALMOST HOME

A CONTEMPORARY GUIDE FOR HEAVEN BOUND BELIEVERS

DEBLEAIRE SNELL

Copyright © 2021 by Debleaire Snell. All rights reserved.

Author: Debleaire Snell
Managing Editor: Dr. Jennifer Patterson
Cover and interior layout design: OA.Blueprints, LLC

No part of this publication may be reproduced, stored in a retrieval system, or transmitted, in any form or by any means, electronic, mechanical, photocopying, recording, or otherwise, without the prior written permission of the copyright holder.

Printed in the United States of America

TABLE OF CONTENTS

Dedication..3
Introduction: Hotel Living.......................................4

Section One: Staying on Course
1. No Matter How It Looks......................................10
2. Heaven is Meant for You....................................16
3. Hell is for Someone Else....................................22
4. Don't Get Tired...28

Section Two: Encouragement
5. No More Death...34
6. No More Bad Days...40
7. No More Harm..47

Section Three: Staying Ready
8. Certain, Not Soon...53
9. Heaven-Meter..61
10. Exchange Rate..68
11. Readiness is Relational....................................73
12. Looking Through the Glass Dimly..................78

Section Four: Pitfalls
13. Materialism...84
14. Soul Ties..91
15. Misappropriation of Values..............................96

DEDICATION

Dedicated in memory of my Grandmother Ethel Smith. In 2020 she took her rest. Cancer was the culprit, but soon cancer will be cancelled. The chasm created by death will soon be bridged. To all who mourn hold fast. We are Almost Home.

INTRODUCTION: HOTEL LIVING

I am a frequent traveler. I've stayed in every possible type of hotel. One church put me in a fleabag hotel that had daily and hourly rates, rings around the tub, a hole in the wall, no vent cover, paper thin walls, dirty bed covers, and a barking dog next door. The air conditioner was left unplugged as a message that there was no heat or air coming in or out of that room. I've also had the opportunity to stay in some of the finest hotel establishments there are—places where the food is great, the room is immaculate, the service is first class, and the view is spectacular. Yet, no matter how luxurious the hotel stays, I never let my heart attach to my temporary dwelling.

I rarely put my clothes in the dresser. For the most part, I function from my suitcase. I have no interest in painting the walls to suit my preferred color preference. I have no desire to hang pictures or art. I don't purchase plants to give life to the room or buy candles to give the room the right aroma. I am friendly and courteous to the housekeepers and hospitality staff, but I am not trying to get to know them in a personal way. I have clarity on the purpose of my hotel stay; it is a temporary dwelling space. I function in a way that allows me to enjoy my time there, while making no plans to stay permanently. I work while I'm there, rest while I'm there, and enjoy the journey while I'm there, but there is a detached indifference to hotel living because my primary objective is always to return home. I never attach myself to a hotel in the same ways that I'm attached to my home. I never invest in a hotel the way I invest in my home. I never rest in a hotel in the same way that I rest when I'm at home. Hotel living is exciting and alluring to some, but to me, it's a placeholder until I can get back home.

If you've ever stayed in a hotel, you can probably relate. The hotel bed may be comfortable, but your best rest is located in the bed at your home. Hotel food may be palatable, but it does not satisfy like the food that comes from your home kitchen. Hotel space is somewhat generic; it's not specific. In the course of a year, hundreds of people will sleep in that bed, shower in that tub, and gargle in that hotel sink. In your home, you create a space that caters to your specific details and preferences. Hotels are great options if you don't have anywhere to call home.

My prayer is that we will treat our sojourn in this world like hotel living. Even if your life today is financially affluent, relationally comfortable, and vocationally satisfying, you must maintain a detached indifference to this life. This world is a temporary dwelling place. Our primary investments are not here. Our loyalty is not to this world. Our affections are centered elsewhere. We move from one season of life to the next looking for a city whose builder and maker is God. My physical address may say Harvest, Alabama, but I consider the New Jerusalem as home. In John 14, Jesus stated that He would have to leave His disciples. Sensing their despair at the thought of His departure He articulated His purpose for leaving: "Do not let your hearts be troubled. You believe in God; believe also in me. My Father's house has many rooms; if that were not so, would I have told you that I am going there to prepare a place for you? And if I go and prepare a place for you, I will come back and take you to be with me that you also may be where I am" (John 14:1-3).

Jesus was giving His disciples hope. This hope was exponentially greater than their limited desire to see Caesar and Rome overthrown. Jesus gave them the assurance that they had a home beyond the sky. They would be co-laborers for a kingdom that would never be succeeded. They were to serve as priests and kings of a kingdom where there are no tiers or hierarchies of importance. He wanted them to begin to fix their appetites and affections on the heavenly reward promised to those who love Him. It is this hope that was to sustain the twelve disciples and all who would follow.

This hope was to sustain them as Christ ascended back to Heaven accompanied by a convoy of angels. The hope of their eternal home was to sustain them in the days when they would lose land and possessions as a result of persecution. This hope was to sustain God's people when they would lose limb, liberty and life under the cruel tyranny of Nero. This hope was to sustain John the Revelator in his old age when he would be banished to a rock called Patmos, never to know the comfort of his earthly home again.

It is this hope that sustains you when death strikes in ways that can be anticipated and when it strikes with the suddenness of the wind. It is our heavenly hope that sustains us when friends are few and enemies grow more by the day. It is this hope that anchors us when disappointment abounds, physical pain afflicts, and depression resists your protest for it to depart. It is the hope of our home beyond the sky that allows us to laugh when we should be crying; it allows us to stand when we feel like lying down; it compels us to keep going when we want to quit; and it allows us to praise when we should be complaining. This hope makes our spirits indomitable and our resilience invincible as we bounce back time and again from every conceivable let-down.

My friends, this world will soon pass away. One day, every mountain will be shaken, every hill will be flattened, every valley will be filled in, the oceans will shake with swelling, and the atmosphere will melt as this life comes to its predicted, apocalyptic conclusion. The great Lord of Glory, Jesus Christ, will come triumphantly yet unanticipated by the masses. For the unredeemed, His appearance will be met with regret-filled lamentations. Their shock will be similar to the fear that grips one's soul when a thief breaks in at midnight. However, the redeemed will look with gladness at the long-awaited Redeemer and with joyful voices they will exclaim, "Lo, this is our God; we have waited for him and he will deliver us" (Isaiah 25:9).

The dead will be snatched from their graves and be re-created in the amount of time that it takes to wink an eye. Bone will gather to bone, limb will reunite with limb, and ashes will regain their premortal form. Grave seals will be broken from the burial place of Adam to the grave of Noah, David, Peter, Paul, John, your grandmother, husband, sibling, and father. Not a single resting spot of the redeemed will be left occupied. Angels who marked the spots where the bodies of the redeemed were hidden or where their ashes were interned will do a miraculous work, gathering the redeemed from the four corners of the earth. Then all who are alive to welcome Jesus back to the earth will have gravity suspended as we are instantly caught up in the clouds to meet the Lord in the air. We will experience a change that invigorates. Mortality will be washed away in the assent and corruption will be removed from the software of our souls.

We will then take a journey toward our heavenly abode. Seraphim and cherubim who excel in strength will open gates of pearls so we can enter into the city. We will be overwhelmed by the breathtaking majesty of the golden streets. A diverse sea of humanity with representation from every kindred, tribe, and tongue will unite their grateful voices in unending praise as they stand on the sea of glass. There will be singing, clapping, rejoicing, shouting, dancing, hugging, and crying as the reunion commences. The first stream of joyful tears will fall as we are reunited with Father, Son, and Holy Spirit. The second stream of joyful tears will fall as we are reunited with loved ones long missed.

We will finally be able to experience soul rest. It eludes us here. We get it in spurts and tiny doses, but in this life, there is constant agitation. Our minds could never be at rest here. The mind has to master past tensions, present tensions, and anticipated tensions. But when we get home, everything that snatches away soul rest will be a distant and permanent memory.

My friends, I believe that we are almost home. This book is a clarion call to Heaven-bound believers. It is designed to encourage, challenge, inform, and clarify where we are in time. My goal is to disturb your satisfaction with this life. My objective is to build your faith to lay claim to the something better that God has prepared. God's Spirit has spoken expressly in these times so that our grip on material things, earthly thinking, and life's treasures might decrease. As I wrote this book, I paced the floor, I cried, I shouted, and my hands trembled. This project did something personal for me. I have been revived and strengthened as God's Word has constantly reminded me that we are almost home.

To be clear, this book is not for the person who sees Heaven as optional. This project is not for somebody who is just hoping to get there. This is a contemporary, spiritual guide for the person who has made a decision to go to Heaven. It is for the individual who is actively making plans to go to Heaven. It is for those who will sacrifice earthly prizes for Heaven. This book will only appeal to people who are willing to live as pilgrims. I wrote this to the weary, hurting soul who refuses to live through this earth's hell and die in an eternal hell. It is for the person who does not just see Heaven as a place, but as a person. What drives you is relationship, not a trouble-free circumstance.

So, let's live out of our suitcases while we're here. Let's not try to customize this life to make ourselves more comfortable. Let's maintain some indifference to the values of the culture. Let's stay slightly detached from the practices that might sway us from pilgrim status to resident. Let's fight off fatigue and weariness with all that is in us. Let us continue to believe, pray, trust, hope, worship, serve, and labor because, believe it or not, we are almost home.

1

NO MATTER HOW IT LOOKS

But we have this treasure in earthen vessels, that the excellence of the power may be of God and not of us. We are hard-pressed on every side, yet not crushed; we are perplexed, but not in despair; persecuted, but not forsaken; struck down, but not destroyed."
2 Corinthians 4:7-9

The year 2020 is one that most people want to forget. This year has been marked by tragedy from the very start. I remember coming home after a long day on the last Sunday in January. I just wanted to kick back and watch a little NBA action. Then social media began to grieve as news of NBA legend Kobe Bryant's death was confirmed. Our hearts were further saddened when it was also confirmed that his 13-year-old daughter, along with several other families, tragically died in a helicopter crash on their way to a basketball game. Many of us thought that this was a terrible way to start the year. We didn't know that was only the beginning of many sorrows to come.

A few weeks into the month of February, we got word of a strange virus that started in China and had begun to spread. The leadership of our country downplayed the virus's effects and its dangerous potential. While I preached at a revival in New Jersey on March 11, the world went into an indefinite lockdown. I watched the news from the airport Marriott in Newark, New Jersey with great anxiety, not knowing whether or not my flight on March 13 would take off and allow me to come back home. We thought that maybe the lockdown would last for a couple of weeks and that life would soon return to normal. We did not realize that nine months later, face coverings would be here to stay, holiday gatherings would be limited, travel would still be restricted, and that 300,000 empty chairs would be at holiday tables.

Memorial Day weekend brought more bad news. Minnesota police officer Derek Chauvin placed his knee on the neck of an African American man named George Floyd, strangling him with cold indifference before visible cameras for eight minutes and forty-six seconds. This tragedy would shine an even greater light on the tragic police killings of Breonna Taylor, Ahmad Arbery, and Rayshard Brooks. The summer months were marked by civil unrest, protest, grief, and cries for change.

Wildfires consumed thousands upon thousands of acres of land in the northwestern part of the country, affecting life and property. The news footage of these events seemed like something John would have seen in vision in the book of Revelation. We were emotionally and mentally badgered as the soul of the nation was defined in our November presidential elections. Through political propaganda, people grew anxious as fear tactics became the chief tool of a failing president determined to stay in power.

What we have wrongly done is blame 2020. In some weird superstitious way, we have applied these tensions and limitations to a single year. Many tweets stated messages like, "We can't wait for this year to be over!" as if 2021 guaranteed something better. The belief is that the dawning of a new year guarantees new hope, new reality, and a semblance of normalcy. Similar to all who have been affected by the pangs of life this year, I hope they are correct. But if I read scripture correctly, the closer we get to the coming of Jesus, these types of years won't become less common; they will become more common. The seven angels that John saw holding back the winds of strife in Revelation are soon to be relieved of their duty. I think it is important that we spiritually brace ourselves for more strife, uncertainty, loss, unrest, and turbulence.

At times when I fly, the captain comes over the loudspeaker and braces the cabin for a season of turbulence. He alerts us that drink services will be temporarily suspended because of turbulence. Passengers are asked to remain seated with seatbelts on and tray tables in the upright, locked position because we are about to go through some turbulence. I used to think that the plane had some type of mechanism or device that could detect atmospheric changes. I assumed that was how they knew there was going to be turbulence.

One day I decided to ask the pilot about this on my way off of my flight. I wanted to know how they knew if there would be turbulence. Was there a device that lets them know that the atmospheric pressure was changing? The captain laughed and shared that it was a lot less complicated than that. He said that all flights travel through the same pathways. He continued by sharing that the way they know there is going to be turbulence is by receiving news that someone else in our same flight path has already gone through it. The captain is alerted by radio. They learn the coordinates of the turbulence and also how rough it is going to be. From there, the captain makes adjustments based on the plane that has already gone through it and has made it through to the other side. They don't get nervous about turbulence because they know those who have already gone through it and have navigated it successfully.

Friends of mine, there are some turbulent times that lie ahead of us. The reason we know this is because our great God has seen what will happen in life all the way down to the end. He has gone ahead of us, operating in the future as if it were the present. He has informed us of the coordinates and the strength of the turbulence. We don't need to fear because He has already gone through it and He is waiting for us on the other side.

Many of us have had to weep a great deal this year. Many of us wept as we said goodbye to employment. Too many have wept because they had to say goodbye to the business they had sacrificed so greatly to establish. Many have had to say goodbye to their health. Many have had to say goodbye to loved ones and have fallen asleep in death. The goodbyes seem incomplete as many were unable to gather to pay their respects and outwardly grieve. The present may seem dark and the future may appear daunting, but I want to caution you not to build your assessment of God's faithfulness based on how things look today. I want to encourage you to position your faith on the forecast, not the outlook.

We were planning an outdoor trip with the kids one weekend. Every day that week, cold hard rain fell endlessly to the ground. The kids asked if we were going to cancel our trip because when they looked out the window, all they saw was rain. Whenever we went to the car, all they saw was rain. I told them that we were still planning to go. They said, "We can't go Daddy, it's raining." They were making their plans for the weekend based on the outlook on Thursday. Later that day, we turned on the news and I let them watch the meteorologist's forecast. He reported that even though it was raining that Thursday, by the time Saturday came, there was sunshine in the forecast. He said, "I know it looks bad today, but the sunshine will be here by the weekend."

Meteorologists, in many ways, are like prophets. They predict when storms will come and when they will go. The reason they can predict storms is that they look at the world from a Doppler radar that gives them a view from up high. They see where the storms originate, and they know the speed at which they travel. Based upon that, they can make an educated guess on when the storm is going to pass through. We can't make that type of assessment from the ground. The rain looks permanent when you're looking up from the ground. The meteorologist knows that the rain is going to pass because he's looking at the world from up high.

I want you to know that God does not look at the world from the ground up. God has an "up high" vantage point. Our great God sits high and looks low. He knows when the storms will arrive and how long they will linger. Because God sits up high, He knows and also determines when the storm is going to pass.

I want to say to the weary, down-trodden, broken person, trouble won't last always. This too will pass. No matter what you see in the outlook, please know that sunshine is in Heaven's forecast. It may be dark here, but when Jesus comes again, we will see the breaking of day.

I want you to hold on to your hope, hold on to your faith, and hold on to God's unchanging hand. When the money is funny, keep holding on. When pain touches your body, hold on. When spouses walk away, hold on. When employment is scarce, hold on. When friends are few and enemies are many, hold on. When your child breaks your heart into 1,000 pieces, keep holding on. When darkness tries to eclipse the light, hold on. When the hill seems too steep, hold on. Come hell or high water, keep holding on because, in a little while, we're going home.

REFLECTION

Review (What struck you personally)?

Revelation (What is God Saying to You)?

Response (What are you going to do today)?

2

HEAVEN IS MEANT FOR YOU

Do not let your hearts be troubled. You believe in God; believe also in me. My Father's house has many rooms; if that were not so, would I have told you that I am going there to prepare a place for you? And if I go and prepare a place for you, I will come back and take you to be with me. Then you will also be where I am.
John 14:1-3

From time to time when I'm out and about, I will see something that I know my kids would like. Because their happiness brings me joy, I'll pick it up for them. I make the purchase with them in mind. I make the buy with the sole intention of giving it to them. When I purchase a gift for them, I don't require them to earn it. The only requirement is that they receive it with gratitude. Even if their behavior is less than stellar, I may hold onto it for a little while, but at some point, I'm going to figure out a way to give it to them. As a father, it does me no good to withhold their gifts. I have no use for Hot Wheels, Beyblades, Mario Kart, or princess sets. My joy is drained if I never get to give them what has been purchased for them.

You are probably wondering what my point is. Because we hold a flawed perception of God, many of us still see

Heaven as unattainable. We view Heaven as an achievement that must be earned as opposed to a gift that must be received. Morally, we see our lives as an audition for the kingdom of Heaven. As I sit with people during end-of-life scenarios, on more than one occasion I've heard people say, "I hope my good outweighs my bad," as if God has been keeping score where His judgment is based on a calculation of your good deeds in contrast to your bad deeds. However, your spot in Heaven cannot earned. Your spot in Heaven needs to be received as a gift. Heaven was prepared for you and with you in mind. Jesus is not trying to figure out ways to keep you out of Heaven. Jesus applied the penalty of sin to Himself so that He could get you into Heaven. While mankind was running and hiding from God, God was working on a plan to ensure that we could make it home.

God desires for us to make it to Heaven so badly that the standard for entrance could not be set any lower. In John 3:16, the Bible says, "God so loved the world that he gave his only begotten son that whosoever believes in him should not perish but have everlasting life." The standard for salvation and heavenly entrance is not perfect behavior; instead, it is perfect belief. God builds on this in Romans 10:9-11: "That if thou shalt confess with thy mouth the Lord Jesus, and shalt believe in thine heart that God hath raised him from the dead, thou shalt be saved. For with the heart man believeth unto righteousness; and with the mouth confession is made unto salvation. For the scripture saith, whosoever believeth on him shall not be ashamed." Heaven's attainability is reiterated in the epistle to the Ephesians, "For it is by grace you have been saved, through faith—and this is not from yourselves, it is the gift of God not by works, so that no one can boast" (Ephesians 2:8-9).

The requirement for Heaven is not behavior, but belief. Belief in the merits of Jesus' sacrifice and laying claim to them allows His righteousness to be put in the place of your wickedness. Receiving Christ's sacrifice on your behalf is all that it takes to gain your ticket and your title to

> **Heaven was prepared for you and with you in mind. Jesus is not trying to figure out ways to keep you out of Heaven. Jesus applied the penalty of sin to Himself so that He could get you into Heaven.**

Heaven. God has made it simple and accessible to all people. Jesus stated, "All that the Father giveth Me shall come to Me: and him that cometh to me I will in no wise cast out" (John 6:37). Heaven and eternal life are gifts that are pre-ordained for us to receive. They were planned for with the hope that we would willingly and enthusiastically participate.

I feel the tension that some of you may experience in response to what you are reading. Your entire life you have been told that you must "do this" and "abstain from that" in order to be saved. The emphasis was on how well you behaved rather than on how much you believed. We are not at odds right now. Some just have the order inverted. We are saved through our belief in Jesus. Our righteous behaviors are an outgrowth of our beliefs in the righteous work of Jesus. Our bad behavior grows out of our unbelief. Behaviors, both good and bad, follow our beliefs. Our behaviors don't create salvation; they authenticate our saving transformation. Your good works are the proof that you truly believe and have been transformed by the power of God.

In the salvation narrative, many have the roles confused. We see Jesus has prosecutor—the One who looks to condemn or apply a guilty sentence. Not true. The Bible identifies Satan as the "accuser" (Revelation 12:10). He is the one who brings charges and condemnation to the people of God. On the other hand, Jesus' role is not to condemn, but to justify.

"It is God who justifies. Who then is the one who condemns? No one. Christ Jesus who died—more than that, who was raised to life—is at the right hand of God and is also interceding for us" (Romans 8:33–34).

"My little children, these things write I unto you, that ye sin not. And if any man sin, we have an advocate with the Father, Jesus Christ the righteous" (1 John 2:1).

> **The reason we have such anxiety about heaven is because we have applied the character traits of Satan to Christ.**

Hallelujah! Jesus is our defender, our advocate, and our mediator. His goal is not to expose us, but to cover us. His design is not to exclude us, but to include us. His desire is not to shame us, but to remove our shame. The reason we have such anxiety about heaven is because we have applied the character traits of Satan to Christ. "The enemy of good blinded the minds of men, so that they looked upon God with fear; they thought of Him as severe and unforgiving. Satan led men to conceive of God as a being whose chief attribute is stern justice—one who is a severe judge, a harsh, exacting creditor. He pictured the Creator as a being who is watching with jealous eye to discern the errors and mistakes of men, that He may visit judgments upon them. It was to remove this dark shadow, by revealing to the world the infinite love of God, that Jesus came to live among men" (Steps to Christ, 10.3).

We live with needless guilt as slaves to the voice of condemnation, thinking that the guilt has been applied by God. Don't be deceived any longer. The condemnation has been leveled by Satan to keep you in Adam's position of hiding and self-covering, separated from the Savior. However, God created Heaven with you in mind. Heaven is for you. Heaven has been reserved for you. There is a seat at the table for you. Make the decision to RSVP today. Heaven will mourn if you are not present. It is time for you to lay claim to the gift that was purchased at so great a price. and do not avoid them. You cannot dictate the terms or timing of God's work, but your normals will radically change when you allow God to finish His work in His way.

REFLECTION

Review (What struck you personally)?

_____
_____
_____
_____

Revelation (What is God Saying to You)?

_____
_____
_____
_____

Response (What are you going to do today)?

_____
_____
_____
_____

3

HELL IS FOR SOMEONE ELSE

Depart from Me, accursed ones, into the eternal fire which has been prepared for the devil and his angels.
Matthew 25:41

Growing up, I heard people say that God is in the miracle-working business. He was described as a heart-fixer, a soul-sustainer, and a mind-regulator. Our great God is certainly all those things. I can attest that He has worked miracles, fixes my heart, sustains my soul, and helps regulate my mind. But His chief occupation is that of redeemer. He is in the soul-saving business. The entire canon of scripture is simply an overview of God's attempt to bridge the gap between Himself and mankind. The objective is to expose the world to God's love. His love is seen from the time He goes searching for mankind in the garden until the day He gives up His breath at Golgotha.

In order to understand God's love and His desire to spend eternity with us, we must have an accurate perception of His character. In scripture, God is described as Creator instead of destroyer. He is called Redeemer, not punisher. He is the God of reconciliation rather than the God of separation. He is man's savior, not man's captor. He is the Messiah, not a masochist.

Jesus is all the way in regarding our redemption. He is

fully invested in our salvation. I would be nervous about salvation if I wanted to go to Heaven and God didn't really want me there. However, in truth, my salvation is simply accepting what God wants for me even more than I want it for myself. When it comes down to deciding whether or not to redeem us, God does not sit as an indifferent judge, objectively weighing evidence. Instead, He is completely partial and totally biased. The bias cuts in our favor. Hallelujah to the Lamb!

Jesus' death on Calvary made provision for all mankind. It must relentlessly burn God's heart that there are so few people who actually take part in this glorious redemption. To be clear, God is not a cuddly bundle of love who is indifferent to law and righteousness. God has the capability and He will eventually exercise the ability to eternally destroy. What I want us to understand is the fact that destruction is not His aim, nor goal. He wants to avoid punishment in the same way that a parent takes no joy in punishing his or her child.

In most cases where a loving parent decides to punish with a belt, switch, time out, or cancelled privileges, it is usually the result of ignored appeal after ignored appeal. Punishment is usually the final resort. In the same way, God will take no joy when the wicked are destroyed. It is His last option. To destroy even one of His children must feel like a self-mangling activity for God. Each and every one of us bears His image and He paid the highest possible price for us all. For a creator, destruction feels counterintuitive. Harming us is like harming Himself. The only agony worse than the Cross is the agony of applying the second death penalty to the unredeemed.

God is an adequate destroyer, but even the Bible describes this as an odd assignment for Him. "For the LORD shall rise up as in mount Perazim, he shall be wroth as in the valley of Gibeon, that he may do his work, his strange work; and bring to pass his act, his strange act" (Isaiah

28:21). The act of destroying His own workmanship seems strange and misplaced for a God dedicated to salvation. "As surely as I live, declares the Sovereign LORD, I take no pleasure in the death of the wicked, but rather that they turn from their ways and live. Turn! Turn from your evil ways! Why will you die, people of Israel?" (Ezekiel 33:11).

I guess what I'm saying is, you were not meant to be lost. Everything in the salvation equation has been tilted for your benefit. In Matthew 25, Jesus makes it very clear that hell's fire was not intended for you; it will be kindled "for the devil and his angels." The lake of fire is unlike anything we know. It is a supernatural arrangement that was not designed to burn wood, cloth, and metal. It is actually a supernatural concoction designed to destroy the presence of sin and spirit beings like Lucifer and his following angels. A fire much less sophisticated would suffice if it were designed with us in mind.

Those who are eternally damned will be crashing a party that they were not invited to. It will be such needless carnage. The punishment won't be a result of them not being good enough. It won't result from them not following the rules accurately enough. Their eternal death is the wages they receive for working so hard to elude salvation over a lifetime. In Romans, eternal life is described as a gift. Romans 6:23 says that the wages of sin are death. Salvation is gifted; destruction is earned. The reason why death and destruction are described as labor is because you have to work really hard to be lost. The energy it takes to elude God

> **To destroy even one of His children must feel like a self-mangling activity for God. Each and every one of us bears His image and He paid the highest possible price for us all. For a creator, destruction feels counterintuitive. Harming us is like harming Himself.**

and resist His invitation, run past His boundaries, and ignore His constant appeals must be rewarded.

The following story is a little bit triggering. I learned the hard way as I shared it on a Wednesday night with my church. I live in the country and my house is adjacent to an open, farmer's field. On mornings when walking out of the garage on the side of my house, I would see a family of rabbits that graced us with periodic visits. It is truly scenic and peaceful to see how comfortable the rabbits had become hanging around by the fence even when they saw us going in and out. However, about a year ago, we had a two-week stretch where it seemed like we were being invaded by field mice in the garage and around the perimeter of the house. My dad sent me some really powerful poison that helped him deal with vermin at his home in Florida, so I strategically placed the poison in chunks around the perimeter of the house. The reason for the poison was to slow down the mouse invasion. The trap was laid out with mice in mind. One day when I pulled into the driveway, I was devastated to see one of the rabbits in the corner nibbling on the poison. I tried to stop the rabbit, but it was too late. He hopped away and unfortunately, never returned. The trap had not been meant for him; it was meant for the unruly, rebellious mice that I wanted to deal with. Our family friend died because it ate poison that was meant for another.

This is what the great judgment day will be like. Those who reject the offer of redemption will suffer Satan's punishment. After the thousand years expires, the New Jerusalem will descend toward this earth while the wicked are raised from the dead. Picking up just where they ceased their schemes, they will begin to charge at the city as it descends. Streams of sulfur and fire will fall with acidic rage on all of God's enemies where they will suffer their final fate. It is on that day that they will finally realize that their loyalty was misplaced, and their choice was eternally erroneous.

This is the horrible end of the wicked. It is awful and it is to be dreaded. The good news for somebody reading today is that there is still time. The offer of salvation still stands. The redemption coupon has not yet expired. If you are in the faith and heading home, don't give up on your journey. Write off fatigue, exhaustion, and earthly distractions as if your life depends on it. Keep pressing and patiently run the race that is in front of you. To those who have yet to submit and say yes to the great invitation of salvation, God is calling out to you today.

Your reading of this chapter is not accidental; it is providential. God is orchestrating this moment. It's up to you to decide what you will do with it. You were created for fellowship with God. You were designed for relationship with the Almighty. There is a mansion in Heaven where an angel waits to inscribe your name. As you sit before the fork in the road of decision, realize that there is a broad road and there is a narrow road. The broad road may have more people, it may seem more exciting, and it may seem full of more adventure; however, you will despise where that road ends. The narrow way may not be as flashy, but on that road you will find peace, joy, contentment, and love that cannot be found anywhere else on this earth. Most importantly, that narrow road will lead you to the Savior's feet. That road will lead you home. Which road will you take today?

REFLECTION

Review (What struck you personally)?

Revelation (What is God Saying to You)?

Response (What are you going to do today)?

4

DON'T GET TIRED

*Let us not become weary in doing good, for at the
proper time we will reap a harvest if we
do not give up.*
Galatians 6:9

There is a particular threat to our journey home that is not often addressed. We tend to be watchful or on guard against obvious threats, so we avoid things like alcohol, drugs, and sexual immorality. However, there is one subtle imperceptible threat that has the capacity to derail many heaven-bound believers. This unseen, unanticipated threat is weariness.

The journey home requires spiritual and emotional fortitude that this life constantly tries to drain from us. Consider some of the imagery that is used to describe the activity of believers. In Philippians 3:12, Paul says, "I press on." The author of the book of Hebrews tells us that we must "run with patience the race that is set before us (Hebrews 12:1). In Luke 13:24, Jesus tells us to "strive to enter through the narrow door." In 2 Timothy 2:3, we are counseled to "endure hardship." In James 1:12, we are told to "persevere under trial." Jesus and the apostles are trying to prepare us for a journey that has the potential to exhaust us. They prepare us with terms like perseverance, pressing, endurance, and striving. Being saved is very easy. Being sanctified is the hard part. Sanctification is a fancy church term. It is simply the process by which Jesus perfectly reduplicates His character in us. This process begins at conversion and it does not end until you die or until Jesus comes.

Those who are being daily sanctified will face outward persecution, Satanic attack, Godly trials, betrayals, disappointment, and loss while being tossed around by the consequences of their own poor choices. Being sanctified is no escape from trouble. It funnels you in the direction of adversity. You can rest assured that you are not alone. "Beloved, do not think it strange concerning the fiery trial which is to try you, as though some strange thing happened to you" (1 Peter 4:12). "We are hard-pressed on every side, yet not crushed; we are perplexed, but not in despair; persecuted, but not forsaken; struck down, but not destroyed" (2 Corinthians 4:8).

In writing to the church in Galatia, Paul penned these words, "Let us not grow weary in well doing, for in due time we will reap a harvest, if we do not give up" (Galatians 6:9). He gave this counsel for a reason. This was not just a Hallmark saying. He wrote in real time to believers in Galatia who had begun to give up. Paul got word that many who were once devout in the faith had begun to backslide simply because they became weary. They began to go back to their former lives because they had not anticipated that the journey with Christ would be so hard. Individuals who had given to the church financially and suffered persecution for their beliefs turned back. Those who had traveled across the land and sea to spread the gospel message began to take their hands off the plow. In Galatia, they went back to their former temples of worship and their previous idols. They went back to lives of drunkenness and revelry. They went back to former chemical substances that brought them temporary peace. They said no to Heaven because the journey home seemed too long, it required too much, and the sacrifices were too many. They were not unconverted, godless, or rebellious; they had simply become weary.

The weariness that I speak of is not physical. It cannot be solved with a nap, vacation, or massage. The weariness that I am addressing is a fatigue that reaches down into the soul. I'm addressing a fatigue that causes the fire to go out. It's the kind of weariness that saps you of the strength to pray. It's the kind of tired that fastens you to your couch or bed only when it's time to go to church. It's a fatigue so great that even when you have the desire to praise God, you lack the strength and the will to carry it out. It's a fatigue that welcomes vices or any chemical shortcuts to peace, tranquility, or numbness. It's a fatigue that makes the preacher's words bounce off of your eardrums so that they take no root in your heart. It's a fatigue that makes Heaven seem so far away that you should just settle for what this life has to offer.

There are times when we misdiagnose what is happening with some of God's people. What we term spiritual indifference, rebellion, or laziness is simply the result of weariness. It's what happens when people give up. I see it often. In baptizing a man or woman, when they come out of the pool, there is a light in their eyes that shines brighter than a thousand suns. Their love for God runs deep and is infectious. After a while, they go back to a home where their faith is not celebrated, to a job where their faith is smothered, and back to friends where their faith is ridiculed. A combination of trials, Satanic attacks, and a few bad breaks over time wearies them. If they don't have an adequate faith community, the fatigue will inevitably get them. I see the same thing with "mature" believers. They grow weary too.

> **There are times when we misdiagnose what is happening with some of God's people. What we term spiritual indifference, rebellion, or laziness is simply the result of weariness.**

The only difference is that mature believers will not leave church or denounce their faith. They will eventually settle for a life where they have a form of godliness with the absence of its power. They pray hollow prayers, sing songs of praise from their lips, but never from their hearts. They grudgingly give and they serve just enough to satisfy an agitated conscious. They don't even realize that their lukewarm, passive Christianity is the result of weariness. There is only one cure for spiritual weariness. For physical weariness, the cure is a good night's rest. For emotional weariness, the cure may be a counseling session or a vacation. But spiritual weariness can only be cast off in one way. You must plug your soul completely into Jesus Christ. You can't just go through the motions of religion. You have to get connected to the source of all spiritual life and vitality. Recently, my wife was playing some music over the speakers in the house as she often does. My daughter picked up the phone to see which song she was playing. She noticed that the battery life of the phone was down to 2%. My wife plugged the phone in to the power outlet and continued to play music without a thought. My daughter came back downstairs and noticed that the iPhone was still playing music nearly an hour later. When she picked it up again, she noticed that the battery life was still at 2%. She began to inquire as to how the phone could still be playing music all of this time at a 2% battery level. My wife simply explained that even though the battery life was down to its last portion, the phone was able to keep functioning because it was plugged in. Even though it was at diminished capacity, it would keep going as long as it was plugged in. The battery life will last indefinitely as long as it is plugged in. It does not matter how little battery life is left as long as it stays plugged in.

To the person who is down to their last 2% of strength, to the one who is at diminished spiritual capacity, or the one who feels like you have nothing left to give, you simply need to make sure that you are plugged all the way into

Jesus Christ. Just like the phone was able to keep going beyond its capacity because it was plugged in, you will be able to go further than you think you can go if you are plugged in to Jesus Christ.

We are rounding the corner. We are coming around the bend. Our redemption draws closer and Heaven is in our view. This is no time to get tired. This is not the season to give up. I charge you to seek God for a second, spiritual wind. We must run our best mile right before we cross the finish line. Fight fatigue. Rebuke weariness. Make your mind up again today to say, "I will not let anything cause me to settle short of making it to my eternal home." You are almost there. Don't let weariness sabotage you.

REFLECTION

Review (What struck you personally)?

_____
_____
_____
_____

Revelation (What is God Saying to You)?

_____
_____
_____
_____
_____

Response (What are you going to do today)?

_____
_____
_____
_____
_____

5

NO MORE DEATH

The last enemy to be destroyed is death.
1 Corinthians 15:26

12/8/2020 12:39pm

I should probably warn you that I am writing from a place of rage today. I'm not sure if it's a good idea; it's just the space that I currently occupy. I'm sitting in my truck at Oakwood Memorial Gardens in Huntsville, Alabama. I'm not here for dramatic affect. I'm here because I'm sick of it. What I'm sick of is death!

I just concluded my fourth funeral in the last seven days. I have another one to officiate four days from now. What triggered my rage is that after we finished lowering the body into the ground, I walked over a few feet and saw the grave of the person we buried last week. As I was walking to my car, every ten feet, I saw the grave of someone else I either knew or assisted in burying. I have had to become too acquainted with death. At times, I can sense his cold, icy presence attempting to draw near to the living in their final days. I'm just sick of it. I'm frustrated. I'm pissed. I'm angry.

I can't explain the numbing techniques I've developed so that I can maintain my composure during funerals as I stand before wives, husbands, siblings, or small children who are lamenting the death of their loved ones. I am constantly adding to the arsenal of self-soothing techniques needed to continue to function during funerals. I'm running out of comforting words to say. More and more, I find myself having to ask God for strength just to walk into a room to sit with a mourning family. I sit here now asking God, "Lord, when will it end?"

12/8/2020 6:00pm
I've had a chance to regroup. The feelings I shared from earlier today do not reflect a meltdown of faith. I simply talked in real time about how death and loss affect all of us. Death is a pernicious intruder, touching all of humanity in some way, shape, or form. Death is accurate and unrelenting. Death is a careful hunter whose skill has been sharpened and perfected by 6,000 years of regular practice. His trophies include patriarchs, prophets, priests, pastors, presidents, prefects, and people of every sort. His arsenal is broad and wide and missing no weapon. He uses sickness, disease, famine, and pestilence. One of his tools is suicide. Another tool is murder. Death uses man's ego as a weapon as well as man's need for supremacy, his need to be exalted, and his need for power.

Death will use your unwillingness to control your appetite, vice, or recklessness to cut you down before your time. He will use youthful curiosity and rebellion to make an early visit on your life. At times, death collaborates with calamity in the form of earthquakes, hurricanes, tornadoes, typhoons, mudslides, volcanoes, or ice storms to bring about sadness. He is present and active in every pool accident and plane crash. He sends text messages that distract drivers, which leads to fatal car wrecks. If he can't make an early entrance, he will simply wait for your mortality to kick in. If he can't beat you, he will simply out-wait you.

Death visits the wealthy and the poor alike. He comes for the aged and the young. He has no regard for your position in life, your status, or your trophies. He is the one agency that makes no distinction between class and caste among human beings. Because of Adam's sin, temporary authority has been yielded over to death. He operates under the direction of Satan, executing Satan's will. He boldly struts about this earth with fear of no man. All of humanity has had to succumb to him and go his way at some point.

However, there is one mar on death's record. There is a blemish on his résumé. There is One whose power he cannot overcome. It is because of that one man that could not be held down by death's grip that we have hope. "Christ has indeed been raised from the dead, the first fruits of those who have fallen asleep. For since death came through a man, the resurrection of the dead also comes through a man. For as in Adam all die, so in Christ all will be made alive. But each in turn: Christ, the first fruits; then, when he comes, those who belong to him" (1 Corinthians 15:20-23).

As Jesus came forth from a Roman tomb, sealed with Pilot's signet and blocked by a massive stone, He became the forerunner of all who would be resurrected from the grave. Paul states that Christ became the "first fruits" of them that sleep. In agriculture after a field has been planted and the seed has germinated before harvest time, there are first fruits that break the ground. The first fruits are evidence that the remaining harvest is safe. The first fruits are proof that the rest of the harvest will break ground. When Jesus broke the ground that Easter Sunday morning, He became evidence that the rest of us that sleep one day would break the ground as He did.

When He came forth from the grave, He took dominion from death and He took the keys of hell back under His authority. Some may bristle against this truth because death still exists. The work that Jesus did at the cross and His resurrection did not nullify the immediate power of death, but it nullified the permanent power of death. The cross and the resurrection removed the sting from death and diluted death's power to an unconscious sleep for the righteous. The temporary sleep will end when the Lord of Glory appears in the clouds with the voice of the Archangel and the trumpet of God. When the trumpet blasts, all who have died in Christ will be raised to an incorruptible state and their mortality will no longer be held under the slavish powers of death.

It is on that day that death will be stripped of all authority. Death himself will be sentenced to death. Captivity will be taken captive and the grave will no longer be permitted to house God's people. Today started out lousy, but now, as the sun has sunk into the west, I sit here revived. Revived because I looked back to the Cross and my hope was renewed through looking again at the resurrected Christ who made death temporary. My hope is revived as I look forward to resurrection morning when all of the redeemed who have rested in Christ will be reunited and redeemed in Him. Every cemetery that is now a place of sorrow and sadness will become a place of rejoicing as the redeemed of all ages break the ground in response to the call of their Savior welcoming them home.

> There are times when we misdiagnose what is happening with some of God's people. What we term spiritual indifference, rebellion, or laziness is simply the result of weariness.

Today, I say to the widow, your weeping will one day come to an end. I say to parents, you will see your Godly child again. I say to the disquieted child, you can rest with assurance that you will see your mother and father again. To the mother who moans the miscarriage of her little ones, those babies will be placed in your arms at the second coming of Jesus Christ. "Christ is coming with clouds and with great glory. A multitude of shining angels will attend Him. He will come to raise the dead, and to change the living saints from glory to glory. He will come to honor those who have loved Him, and kept His commandments, and to take them to Himself. He has not forgotten them nor His promise. There will be a relinking of the family chain. When we look upon our dead, we many think of the morning when the trump of God shall sound, when 'the dead shall be raised incorruptible, and we shall be changed.' A little longer, and we shall see the King in His beauty. A little longer, and he will wipe all tears from our eyes. A little longer, and He will present us 'faultless before the presence of His glory with exceeding joy.' Wherefore, when He gave the signs of His coming, He said, 'When these things begin to come to pass, then look up, and lift up your heads; for your redemption draweth nigh'" (Desire of Ages, pg. 632).

REFLECTION

Review (What struck you personally)?

Revelation (What is God Saying to You)?

Response (What are you going to do today)?

6

NO MORE BAD DAYS

He will wipe every tear from their eyes. There will be no more death or mourning or crying or pain, for the old order of things has passed away.
Revelation 21:4

This life is filled with unrelenting disappointment, sorrow, and pain. Our sorrow is so constant that we have built up an unconscious tolerance to it. We are so accustomed to bad days, that we subconsciously brace ourselves for them. I often hear husbands talk about how they put on emotional armor before they leave home to help shield them from the attacks of the day. At times, I find myself tensing up before I turn on the news because I need to ready my heart for the barrage of woes that will be reported. I will admit that I am always a little nervous whenever the phone rings after 9:00 pm because, as a pastor, it usually means news of some type of tragedy. I was recently walking through an office building where I witnessed an employee in her cubicle doing deep breathing exercises in an attempt to get centered so that she could handle what the day was about to bring.

As a believer, perhaps you begin the day by praying for strength. That prayer is needed because you know that life is going to attempt to drain you. You probably pray for wisdom and discernment. That prayer is needed because life is going to present conundrums and confusion. You ask God to protect you. That prayer is needed so that you can be sheltered from the spiritual or physical attacks that bring daily threats. You probably pray for God to sustain you. That prayer is needed because life will confront you with a myriad of circumstances that simply makes you want to give up.

Whether we know it or not, we are actively bracing for bad days. It is an involuntary reflex and protective measure. Bad days are so frequent and so routine that we would be foolish not to anticipate them. In some way, we are bracing for the stresses that our jobs bring. We are trying to manage the unrest and worry that we have about our financial predicaments. Some of you are working through the ugly truth that you hate the marriage that you have committed your entire life to. For many, your days are tedious because you have chronic pain afflicting some part of your body or unseen disease wreaking havoc on vital organs. For others, bad days are all they can perceive as depression suffocates any remnants of joy that God provided with the strength of a python. Someone is reading this with a heavy heart as each day seems grayer than the next because the partner that used to lay next to you in the bed now rests in a cemetery.

Even if the bad day is not yours, you are affected by the suffering that is in this world. As a human community, we intentionally and unintentionally share one another's sorrows. I have not lost anyone to gun violence, but I am saddened with those who have. I don't have cancer; however, I am weighed down with hurt for those who do. Human trafficking has not touched my home, yet I mourn with the victims of such all around me. I have not lost anyone to the coronavirus, but the whole atmosphere is poisoned by grief for those who have. I don't suffer discrimination due to my gender, but I hurt for all of the women in my life who do. Today, I have gainful employment, but I am also burdened for those who do not. Good or bad days are not just evaluated by what has happened to you individually; you also weigh the things that are happening in the world.

Bad days don't discriminate. Bad days come to every race. Bad days visit every gender. Bad days touch the rich and the poor alike. Sometimes bad days come in bunches and they tax the soul with the force of a flood. At times they are spread out but are still present. Sometimes you can see some bad days coming, and other times they make unwelcome visits without the courtesy of an appointment. Even our "good days" are not perfect; it just means that our tensions were a bit more manageable. Even a good day is marred by some type of inconvenience, whether it's traffic on the way home, a mean word spoken, or a negative exchange with the store clerk. On planet earth, bad days are inevitable. Bad days are just one of our accepted normals.

I do want to share a bit of good news. There will come a day, when there will be no more bad days. My mouth can hardly speak it, my hands can hardly write it, and my mind can hardly conceive it. Oh, what great joy awaits us on the other side of this life. On this earth we adjust to unrelenting sadness. In Heaven we will have to make the adjustment to unrelenting joy. On this earth we have to brace ourselves for floods of tragedy, but when we get to Heaven, we will have to brace ourselves for floods of joy, peace, and uninterrupted contentment. Look at how the prophet Isaiah describes the joys of eternal life:

"Then will the eyes of the blind be opened and the ears of the deaf unstopped. Then will the lame leap like a deer, and the mute tongue shout for joy. Water will gush forth in the wilderness and streams in the desert. The burning sand will become a pool, the thirsty ground bubbling springs. In the haunts where jackals once lay, grass and reeds and papyrus will grow. And a highway will be there; it will be called the Way of Holiness; it will be for those who walk on that Way. The unclean will not journey on it; wicked fools will not go about on it. No lion will be there, nor any ravenous beast; they will not be found there. But only the redeemed will walk there, and those the LORD has rescued will return. They will enter Zion with singing; everlasting joy will crown their heads. Gladness and joy will overtake them, and sorrow and sighing will flee away" (Isaiah 35:6-10).

At times, the promise feels unreal and too good to be true. Can you imagine starting the day without the need to brace yourself? When we get home, there will never be another conflict. Can you imagine no longer needing to defend yourself, prove yourself, or make your point? I can hardly fathom a time when no one tries to gain supremacy based on the color of his or her skin, gender, wealth, or pedigree.

Can you imagine days without any physical pain? When we get home, you will never need another aspirin because your head will never hurt. You will never need an asthma inhaler because your breath will be endless. You will never take another insulin injection because your organs will no longer be threatened. You will never be wearied by another chemotherapy session because cancer will be canceled. You will never need a knee brace to run or a walker to walk because your limbs will be as spry as a deer. You won't need Tums or Pepto Bismol because your stomach will never hurt. You won't need Alka-Seltzer or Tylenol because your nose will never run. You won't need aids to hear or glasses to see. All of the aids that help us negotiate physical lack will be rendered obsolete because this mortal will be made immortal by the fulfillment of the promise of our eternal home.

Can you imagine no more emotional pain? There won't be any Kleenex in Heaven because weeping won't be necessary. In Heaven, husbands won't leave wives, neither will parents leave their children. In Heaven, there are no widows or orphans because death will be but a distant memory. In Heaven, there is no loneliness for, whether married or single, we embrace each other as one community of perfect love without tiers or social distinction.

In Heaven there is no depression because the power of sin, which brings a heavy yoke to the soul, will be permanently lifted. In Heaven, there is no emotional scar tissue because there is no bullying, molestation, rape, slavery, trafficking, or abuse. Captivity will be taken captive and Satan, the author of all of these kinds of abuses, will be repaid for every affliction that he has placed on God's children. As the righteous are transported from earth to glory, we will leave every tear of sad lamentation on this earth because sadness will not be permitted to adorn the home that God has prepared for those who love Him. Can you imagine a home with no stress? I can't even fathom a life without some tension or worry. We have been on guard for so long that a worry-free life seems odd to me. Your brain will never have to brace itself for bad news. Your heart will never be visited with anxiety. Your soul will never have to adjust to loss, financial tension, unemployment, family drama, or the day-to-day woes of life. I pray that as you're reading that you can share in the excitement that I feel as I write. My hands tremble as I pen these words. It seems too good to be true. What joyful expectation is ours! We inherited a curse that we didn't create through Adam's sin. However, through Christ's sacrifice, we inherited a promise that we could never, ever deserve. This world and all of its curses are temporary. My prayer is that you hear what the Spirit is saying to the church today. No matter what this day or season of days may bring to you, there will come a day, unknown to us, when we will have our last, bad day. We have something greater to look forward to. In our eternal home, free and unmarred by Adam's curse, we can live the life that God originally planned for us when He moved creation from imagination to reality. So, let us not give up because of bad days. Instead, let us use every bad day as fertilizer. Use every bad day as fuel for the kingdom. Use every bad day as a reminder that this world is not our home.

We have been created for something better. We were created to experience eternal union with the Lord Jesus

> **So, let us not give up because of bad days. Instead, let us use every bad day as fertilizer. Use every bad day as fuel for the kingdom. Use every bad day as a reminder that this world is not our home.**

Christ in a world untouched by sin and its curse. This is the hope that brings joy to my heart. This is the belief that illuminates me during long, dark days. This is the truth that anchors me when waves crash over my soul. It may seem too hard to fathom or too dangerous to grab hold of. It is why Paul in his declaration to the church states, "Eye has not seen, nor ear heard, nor have entered into the heart of man the things which God has prepared for those who love Him" (1 Corinthians 2:9). Thank God almighty that we are almost home.

REFLECTION

Review (What struck you personally)?

_____
_____
_____
_____

Revelation (What is God Saying to You)?

_____
_____
_____
_____

Response (What are you going to do today)?

_____
_____
_____
_____

7

NO MORE HARM

They will neither harm nor destroy on all my holy mountain, for the earth will be filled with the knowledge of the LORD as the waters cover the sea.
Isaiah 11:9

One of the sweet promises of our eternal home is the final elimination of threat. Never again will you have to lock doors. Looking over your shoulder won't be necessary. In Heaven, security systems are not needed, and surveillance cameras will be rendered obsolete. There will be no need for a safe or a lock box. No weapon of self-defense will be needed once we cross the threshold to glory. Neither gun, knife, shank, pipe, mace, taser, nor stick will be permitted in Heaven. The reason they are not needed is because the spirit that engineered their conception will no longer exist.

In Heaven, we will regain the harmony forfeited by Adam and Eve. Our souls will be able to rest because the element of strife will be contained. After Adam's fall, the world's energy shifted in a dark and permanent way. Everything in nature pivoted from a posture of being sustained to a self-preserving posture of survival. For both man and beast, making it through the day became a priority. Their daily hunt was not for sport, but rather for survival. Animals in a Darwinistic push for supremacy migrated into tribalistic behavior in the hope of self-preservation. Lions formed prides so that they could stage attacks on hyenas together. Cheetahs ran in groups to stave off the attacks of jackals. Zebras travelled in cliques of their own kind to keep from being overwhelmed by leopards. Giraffes migrated in tribes to avoid the predatory prowess of female lions looking to feed their cubs. There is no longer harmony in nature. Instantly, the need to survive places everyone in a hierarchy based upon strength in a desperate need to make it one more day.

> Everything in nature pivoted from a posture of being sustained to a self-preserving posture of survival.

However, as sin progressed, the need to survive mutated into the need to be first and most powerful. As human beings began to populate the world, we followed animal instincts. We too began to divide into tribes, first as a survival mechanism, then as a means of procuring and maintaining dominance. We began to segregate ourselves into various tribes based on race, gender, and in some parts of the world, class systems or castes.

> However, as sin progressed, the need to survive mutated into the need to be first and most powerful.

In order to be first or maintain supremacy, we created constructs like slavery, trafficking, indentured servitude, polygamy, and the development of kingdoms. We begin to attach value to persons based upon family heritage, financial worth, skin color, and beauty. Our natures became so demented and savage that by the time we get to Noah's generation, the Bible describes the earth as "filled with violence." Our instincts had become so savage that if God had not intervened with a flood, self-annihilation was the inevitable end. Had the flood not allowed humanity to reset, the righteous line of Seth would have been eliminated, subsequently destroying even the possibility of a Messiah. It was the flood that guaranteed the first coming of Jesus, which makes His second coming possible and guarantees that we can make it home.

The flood gave us a clean slate because it permitted us a chance to start over. But we have learned nothing from our antediluvian predecessors. Greed, selfishness, jealousy, envy, and insecurity drive us to function in the most debased and inhumane ways toward one another. In some parts of the world, young girls are snatched, and their innocence stripped as they are sentenced to lives of work in the sex slave trade—sometimes even before their sexual organs have reached maturity. Tribalism is so strong that in our inner cities, young men shoot one another down in loyalty to the gang colors they represent. The need for supremacy is so great that under Hitler's regime, Jews were subject to genocide while for 400 years, Africans in America were lynched, hung, and beaten bloody so that the thought of revolt could not gain traction. Our threat assessment is so high that when walking through an airport, bags must be checked, shoes must be removed, bottles must be thrown away, and computers must be scanned to avoid the possibility of men taking over planes and flying them into government buildings. We rob, we kill, we steal, we oppress, we war, and we maim for causes that have no moral worth, virtue, or nobility. It is the outworking of our selfishness that is par for the course in the world that Adam left for us.

As a result, we sleep with one eye open. In certain neighborhoods, people can hardly sleep at all. We have to watch our own backs. We buy handguns because of the possibility that someone is willing to do the unthinkable to us in an attempt to take what is ours. There is no cure, no vaccine, and no antidote for this disease. Our sin cannot be cured; it can only be destroyed by hell fire.

The great news is that this level of threat is temporary. The need to harm or be protected from harm will soon expire. When our hero, Jesus, pierces the stratosphere with immortality in His left hand and incorruption in His right hand, He will give man a new nature that is thoroughly drained of this world's poison. Not only will Jesus Christ put an end to human harm, He gives us the guarantee that it will never repeat itself. Through the prophet Nahum, the Word teaches us that "affliction will not rise up a second time" (Nahum 1:9). Never again will a man strike his neighbor. Never again will one have the impulse to take what is not his or hers. The desire to be exalted will be abased. And the need to segregate into our various tribes based upon color, gender, status, or creed for safety will be removed as we function in the earth made new as a kaleidoscope of color. We will join together as a choir of races, singing one song, making one sound, and praising one God with the song of Moses and the Lamb. In the new earth, this harmony will not just be seen among human beings, but also animals. Isaiah sees nature also following suit:

"The wolf will live with the lamb,
the leopard will lie down with the goat,
the calf and the lion and the yearling together;
and a little child will lead them.
The cow will feed with the bear,
their young will lie down together,
and the lion will eat straw like the ox.
The infant will play near the cobra's den,
and the young child will put its hand into the viper's nest.
They will neither harm nor destroy
on all my holy mountain,
for the earth will be filled with the knowledge of the Lord
as the waters cover the sea"
(Isaiah 11:6-9).

Don't you look forward to the day when you can finally feel safe? I long for the day when I can finally be free. I long for the day when I can experience true brotherhood in the human family. I've come to accept that it cannot happen here. No matter how lofty our aims, the power of sin will not let it be so. We will have unity spurts like what we saw after the murder of George Floyd. However, like every season of revival, it comes to an end and people revert back to their various corners and old ways. We will only experience true rest as a people when we can finally function as one people knowing that the need to harm has been buried under the shambles of this world when Jesus Christ comes to carry us home. I don't know about you, but it's time to pack our bags and time to leave them by the door. It's time to ready ourselves for the transition. Help is on the way as our redemption gets closer. I don't know about your but I can't wait to get home.

REFLECTION

Review (What struck you personally)?

_____
_____
_____
_____
_____

Revelation (What is God Saying to You)?

_____
_____
_____
_____
_____

Response (What are you going to do today)?

_____
_____
_____
_____
_____

8

CERTAIN, NOT SOON

But about that day or hour no one knows, not even the angels in heaven, nor the Son, but only the Father.
Mark 13:32

Jesus has been gone for a long time. In fact, He's been gone for roughly 2,000 years. Every generation of believers has expected His return in their lifetime. The apostles died believing that Jesus would come back before they went to their graves. He told the apostle John, "Behold I come quickly and my reward is with me to give to every man according to what his work shall be" (Revelation 22:12). Jesus told John that twenty centuries ago. I don't know about you, but I wouldn't categorize two millennia as quickly.

The long wait for Jesus' return was destined to give rise to doubters about the truthfulness of the claim. Peter predicted that the rise in skepticism would become more intense the longer it took Jesus to return. "They will say, where is this coming He promised? Ever since our ancestors died, everything goes on as it has since the beginning of creation" (2 Peter 3:4). I've been hearing that Jesus is soon to come since I was about 11 years old and I am now 43. Depending on how long you have believed, you've been hearing it even longer. The apostles died waiting for His return. The reformers died waiting for His return. The Adventist pioneers died waiting for His return. Our great-grandparents died waiting for Him to return. We are dying, waiting for His return. Maybe we should stop saying

> **Maybe we should stop saying that Jesus is soon to come and say Jesus is certain to come. Perhaps our hope should be in the assurance of His return instead of the timing.**

that Jesus is soon to come and say Jesus is certain to come. Perhaps our hope should be in the assurance of His return instead of the timing.

Jesus actually tried to make it clear that He would be gone for a long time. In the parable of the ten virgins, the lengthy wait was symbolized in the delay of the bridegroom (Matthew 25:5). We tend to notice the five foolish virgins who bought no oil. The reason they did not bring oil is because they didn't anticipate having to wait so long. They assumed the bridegroom would come right away. Perhaps the parable is not about oil. Possibly, it is about the importance of knowing how to wait.

The lengthy wait for Jesus' return is also foreshadowed in the parable of the talents.

This parable is not about talents in the contemporary definition of the word. A talent was a quantity of money. In the parable, the master dispersed talents to each of his servants based upon their ability to steward the resources given them. The servants were to engage the market and bring the master back a yield on the return. When the master came back, he planned to settle accounts and reward each servant based on his faithfulness or lack thereof. What we usually classify as a parable about how we use our gifts is actually a parable about how we are to wait for Jesus' return: "For *the kingdom of heaven* is like a man traveling to a **far country**, *who* called his own servants and delivered his goods to them. And to one he gave five talents, to another two, and to another one, to each according to his own ability; and immediately he went on a ***journey***. Then he who had received the five talents went and traded with them, and made another five talents. And likewise he who had received two gained two more also. But he who had received one went and dug in the ground, and hid his lord's money. After a long time the lord of those servants came and settled accounts with them. "So he who had received five talents came and brought five other talents, saying, 'Lord, you delivered to me five talents; look, I have gained five more talents besides them.' His lord said to him, 'Well done, good and faithful servant; you were faithful over a few things, I will make you ruler over many things. Enter into the joy of your lord.' He also who had received two talents came and said, 'Lord, you delivered to me two talents; look, I have gained two more talents besides them.' His lord said to him, 'Well done, good and faithful servant; you have been faithful over a few things, I will make you ruler over many things. Enter into the joy of your lord'" (Matthew 25:14-23).

Again, Jesus foreshadowed the lengthy wait for His return by two statements that leap from the pages of scripture. He described the master as going on a "long journey." The master did not come back quickly as Jesus said that the master would return "after a long time." The two parables communicate the coming of a bridegroom and the return of a master. The problem with foolish virgins is that they didn't anticipate a long wait. They were left behind because they didn't have enough oil to withstand the season of darkness that comes during delays. The man with one talent received judgment. The judgment is not a result of a lack of production; instead, it is the result of a lack of activity. Rather than constantly laboring like the man with five talents or the man with two, he buried his talent and as soon as the master left, he spent the remainder of the time watching for the master's return instead of doing the work the master assigned him to do. Instead of focusing on when the master is going to return, we should just focus on the work the master has given us to do.

During the summer months as a teenager, I worked at Florida State University doing odd jobs. I worked a tedious job, building blinds and screens in the basement of the girls' dormitory. Being only a teenager, it was hard working from 8:00 am to 4:30 pm. I couldn't wait until 4:00 pm when our crew leader returned to pick us up so that we could get ready to go home. I noticed something after several weeks of working. The more I sat and watched the clock, the slower the day went by. The more I monitored the time, the more the time seem to drag on. When I assumed a posture of waiting, those eight hours felt more like 80 hours. Through trial and error, I learned that instead of waiting and watching, I should apply my focus to working. If I set a large work goal for the day and poured my energy into my work, before I knew it, the day would be over and my boss would be back to get me so that I could go home.

> **If we are truly sick of the waiting, the cure is for us to keep working. Theologically, we must understand that our wait can't end until our work is complete.**

Perhaps this last day generation should do less sky-watching and more working. There is an assignment that God has given us to do. We should put both hands on the gospel plow and commit ourselves fully to sharing the hope of salvation with an unbelieving world. If we are truly sick of the waiting, the cure is for us to keep working. Theologically, we must understand that our wait can't end until our work is complete. Fundamentally, you must understand what Jesus is waiting on:

"The Lord is not slow in keeping his promise, as some understand slowness. Instead he is patient with you, not wanting anyone to perish, but everyone to come to repentance" (2 Peter 3:9).

"And this gospel of the kingdom will be preached in the whole world as a testimony to all nations, and then the end will come" (Matthew 24:14).

Do you get it? In many ways, we are the cause of the delay. Our indifference toward lost people is the reason He can't come. He is "long-suffering; not willing that anyone should perish." The gospel of the kingdom must travel the world so that all might have an opportunity to say yes or no to the offer of salvation. The gospel must travel across Russia and into the bowels of China. It must saturate India, spread like a virus through Australia, and revive these United States. The sooner we get to work, the shorter we will have to wait.

Why is this so critical? In order to understand the critical nature of the gospel work, you must understand why Jesus is coming back. Even though the master of the house in Matthew 25 was gone for a long time, it was guaranteed that he would return no matter how long he had been away. He went away on business. He had work to complete in another place. No matter how critical his out-of-town assignments were, he must come back to collect on his investments. He left valuables behind. He left personal possessions that were of great worth to him. The reason he couldn't stay away was because his valuable assets were back at home. His valuables demanded that he return.

How do I know that Jesus is coming again? I know He is coming again because of what He left behind. His valuables are here. His greatest investment is here. What matters most to Him is still here on planet Earth. This is not a reference to mountain peaks, green valleys, or blue oceans. His most valuable possessions are the human beings created in His image—the ones who bear His imprint. He must come back to receive the ones that He gave His very life to save. The price He paid was too high for Him to leave us here. The investment is too great for us to be left behind. God values us too much to remain away from us.

"When I consider your heavens,
the work of your fingers,
the moon and the stars,
which you have set in place,
what is mankind that you are mindful of them,
human beings that you care for them?
You have made them a little lower than the angels
and crowned them with glory and honor.
You made them rulers over the works of your hands;
you put everything under their feet" (Psalms 8:3-6).

I hope you're getting it by now. As humans, we stand in awe of other facets of creation. We are wowed by a mountain's strength, awed by a cloud's majesty, impressed by an ocean's depth, and captivated by the sun's fury. We revere the snake's movements and the elephant's power. While all other entities in creation were spoken into being with words, man was crafted by hand, formed with detail and divine precision. You matter to God more than anything else in creation. It is His love for you that summons Him to race through the cosmos to carry you home.

You know what people value by what they leave behind and what they come back to claim. I teach part time at my alma mater, Oakwood University. At the end of class, my students usually dart out of the classroom. In a hurry to get to the next class or just to get away from me, they sometimes leave things behind. At times I will wait for them to return based on what was left. If they leave a pencil or pen behind, I'm not waiting because I know they're not coming back for that. If they leave a t-shirt behind, I'm not waiting because they're not coming back for that. But if they leave an iPhone or an iPad behind, I will wait because I know it will just be a matter of time before they come back to reclaim it. They have paid so much for the iPad or iPhone that they can't simply dismiss it or leave it behind. The investment was so great that their return is guaranteed.

May I suggest that your price tag is greater than that of an iPhone or an iPad Pro? Your value to God is exponentially greater. Jesus has paid such a high price and He cannot leave you here; He must come back and receive you to Himself. You are His greatest asset and His most meaningful investment. I know it's been a long time and you're tempted to get weary. Instead of waiting and watching, commit yourself to working and serving. Rest with the assurance that His love for you will one day summon Him back to this earth where He can retreive His major investment.

REFLECTION

Review (What struck you personally)?

___

Revelation (What is God Saying to You)?

___

Response (What are you going to do today)?

___

9

HEAVEN-METER

Therefore, if you have been raised together with Christ, seek the things that are above, where Christ is sitting at the right hand of God. Set your affection on the things that are above, and not on the things that are on the earth.
Colossians 3:1-2

I have an Apple Watch. The reason I like the watch isn't because it tells me the time. It's not because it allows me to send text messages or because it plays music. I like it because it helps me monitor my fitness goals and progress. When I look at my watch, it lets me know how many steps I've taken. It tells me how many calories I've burned. It shows me my heart rate. I can track the intensity of the day's exercise and compare it with how I performed the day before.

I like things that help me track how well I'm performing. In our journey toward the kingdom of God, we need something that helps us monitor our progress. We need an authentic barometer that alerts us when we are falling short of our spiritual and heavenly goals. For most people, from a spiritual perspective, our lives are a lot of guesswork. The reason we have to guess is because we don't really know how to track movement or monitor our progress. But there are some principles that Jesus gave that allow us to form our own Heaven-meter.

Treasure Location

If you want to track your heavenly progress, the first thing you need to look at is where you are storing your treasure. Jesus plainly stated, "Do not store up for yourselves treasures on earth, where moths and vermin destroy, and where thieves break in and steal. But store up for yourselves treasures in heaven, were moths and vermin do not destroy, and where thieves do not break in and steal" (Matthew 6:19). We are cautioned not to make our greatest investments in rotting material.

Your greatest investment should not be in your garage, closet, pantry, china cabinet, or on your wall. The reason Jesus does not want us to make such great investments there is because those things are so temporary. No matter how expensive the shoes or sweater might be, in a season or two they will be out of style. No matter how sophisticated the automobile is, at some point, it's parts will rust and break down. No matter how long the valuable art piece has been in the family, at some point, it will be placed in the hands of a youthful generation that sees no value in it. Everything manmade is susceptible to rust, dust, rot, ruin, decay, and expiration.

Jesus is calling us to make investments that don't lose their value with time. Timeless investments are made in people. Acts of compassion, mercy, and generosity are heavenly investments. The question of how to store treasure in Heaven is often asked. The poor are God's bank account. The suffering are His safety deposit box. The underprivileged and neglected are His safe. When I make deposits

> **The poor are God's bank account. The suffering are His safety deposit box. The underprivileged and neglected are His safe.**

into people who are created in the image of God and purchased with His blood, the kingdom of Heaven is increased. "Whoever is kind to the poor lends to the LORD, and he will reward them for what they have done" (Proverbs 19:17).

Compassion is not seasonal. Mercy never goes out of style. Generosity is not susceptible to rust, moth, or vermin. Jesus counts our compassion to the suffering as an act done for Him.

"Then the King will say to those on his right, 'Come, you who are blessed by my Father; take your inheritance, the kingdom prepared for you since the creation of the world. For I was hungry and you gave me something to eat, I was thirsty and you gave me something to drink, I was a stranger and you invited me in, I needed clothes and you clothed me, I was sick and you looked after me, I was in prison and you came to visit me.' "Then the righteous will answer him, 'Lord, when did we see you hungry and feed you, or thirsty and give you something to drink? When did we see you a stranger and invite you in, or needing clothes and clothe you? When did we see you sick or in prison and go to visit you?' "The King will reply, 'Truly I tell you, whatever you did for one of the least of these brothers and sisters of mine, you did for me'" (Matthew 25:34-40).

Most people distinguish wicked and righteous by their sin patterns. Jesus measures righteousness and wickedness a little differently. Compassion is the barometer for righteousness

{ **Generosity is a mirror. Selfishness is also a mirror. Your level of generosity or selfishness reveal who you are to the world, to God, and to yourself. Both traits shine light on what you prioritize.** }

and mercy is the measuring stick for holiness. If all of your investments are in you, your Heaven-meter is probably in a dangerously low position.

To be clear, giving to the poor or underprivileged doesn't save us. It doesn't give us brownie points with God. Kindness does not allow you to generate merit points with the Savior. Generosity is a mirror. Selfishness is also a mirror. Your level of generosity or selfishness reveal who you are to the world, to God, and to yourself. Both traits shine light on what you prioritize. Your clinched fist and self-indulgent idolatry don't cause you to be lost. They are evidence that you were already lost. Where you store your treasure is a part of your Heaven-meter.

Where Are Your Affections
The Bible tells us that we are to set our affections on things above. The word "set" suggests that this has to be an intentional work. Our sinful natures create such strong spiritual drifts that our hearts migrate away from heavenly things in an involuntary way. My flesh is going to automatically default to certain settings. By default, it will set itself on earth-centered principles like lust, greed, jealousy, envy, pettiness, and selfishness. My affections will never set themselves on heavenly things. I must choose to daily fix my affections on things that are eternal. Daily, the flesh must be nullified through a fresh infilling of the Holy Spirit. Only then can my desires, appetites, and affections be retrained to receive spiritual things.

One way that we keep our hearts set on things above is that we've got to make sure our entire lives are pulling in the same direction. At times, through the content we meditate on each day, we create our own spiritual conflicts by nullifying the power we asked the Spirit to give us. We struggle as we seek to feed the spiritual man for about ten minutes at the start of the day and we feed the carnal man a steady diet of nutrients for the remainder of the day. You start the day with worship to God. But your

> **Because we are bi-spiritual, we have an orientation to the Spirit of God and the spirit of Satan. We also go both ways. We cannot commit to either side. We cannot be fully devoted to Jesus because we still have an orientation to the things of the flesh.**

music choices are anti-God. Your entertainment works against the things of God. Your conversations do not reflect God. You become a personal tug-of-war when you give access to both sides.

We struggle to keep our hearts set on spiritual things because we are what I call bi-spiritual. We are more familiar with the term bisexual. It is a gender orientation of a person that has affection for both men and women. They go both ways. Because we are bi-spiritual, we have an orientation to the Spirit of God and the spirit of Satan. We also go both ways. We cannot commit to either side. We cannot be fully devoted to Jesus because we still have an orientation to the things of the flesh. This is what makes it so hard for us to keep our hearts fixed on things above. The placement of your affections should let you know where you are on your Heaven-meter.

This chapter is not designed to be exhaustive. There are other things to consider including how you spend your time, your conversation, your commitments, and your financial stewardship. These are all part of your Heaven-meter. Begin here: monitor generosity and look hard at what your affections are sticking to. They reveal a substantial picture of what you consider home and they foreshadow the location of your eternal home.

We don't have to guess. We don't have to be in the dark. Our direction determines our destinations. This chapter may require some serious reformation. I hope this is a blunt and sour wake-up call. Seek the Lord for true revival of heart. Out of that revival and reformation, move toward generosity, kindness, and heavenly affection.

REFLECTION

Review (What struck you personally)?

Revelation (What is God Saying to You)?

Response (What are you going to do today)?

10

EXCHANGE RATE

For our citizenship is in heaven, from which we also eagerly wait for the Savior, the Lord Jesus Christ.
Philippians 3:20

I once preached a revival overseas. When preaching for an extended period of time, your heart can really begin to bond with an audience over the course of a week. After church, you get to spend powerful time counseling people and praying for others. As a result, people have very kind ways that they like to show their appreciation. At times, a mother of the church may knit something. In other instances, a kind person may bring a warm meal for me to eat at the hotel. When people are blessed as they receive, they want to show gratitude in some way.

On this particular preaching experience, I met an older lady who approached me at the end of my final night. She moved through the crowd with a wrinkled envelope in her hand. As she approached me, she thanked me for my ministry then pressed the envelope into my hand. She said, "Pastor, I want to give you $10,000." I was absolutely jarred that she would consider giving such a gift. After my mind quickly raced through a number of items that I could purchase with that money, I quickly came to myself. I felt very uncomfortable accepting a gift of this size from this woman who, in appearance, did not seem to be a person of great means. As I formed my lips to return the gift, the elder beside me cut me off. He said, "Before you do that, let me talk to you." He pulled me aside and informed me that it would be very rude not to receive the lady's gift. I expressed my concern about accepting a gift of this size from one of their elderly members. He shook his head in laughter and said, "Pastor, don't be deceived by the amount. You're thinking as an American and what that amount is worth under your government. But, once you get back home and they convert the check, the exchange rate is going to reduce that amount down to a little under $100. The value may seem high before conversion, but its value will change after conversion." My heart was returned to ease as we both had a good laugh together.

It is amazing how something can seem to have such great value under one government, then once it undergoes conversion, has little value under another government. What may seem to have great value on one side of the ocean may have less value on the other side. The same is true in the spiritual realm. There are things that may seem to have great value before we are converted, but once we are converted those things have less value. There are things that seem to have great worth when we were under Satan's authority. Those things have very little worth now that we are under God's authority. Worldly things have a poor exchange rate once we acquire our citizenship in Heaven.

This is why Jesus asked the following piercing questions, "What good is it for someone to gain the whole world, yet forfeit their soul? Or what can anyone give in exchange for their soul?" (Mark 8:36-37). These might be the two most loaded questions ever posed. These questions bypass all pleasantries and small talk and they get right to the heart of the matter.

As you read this, I want you to soberly contemplate these questions. What would you give in exchange for your soul? What profit is there if you gain all of this world's possessions if you are ultimately lost and left outside the gates of the New Jerusalem. Money feels like a poor exchange for your soul. Your addictions are a horrible exchange for your soul. No set of friends is worth losing your soul. Having bed company is a poor exchange for your soul. No amount of notoriety is a good exchange for your soul. And yet we make these foolish exchanges on a daily basis.

We prioritize perishable things above the imperishable. We attach more value to temporary status than we do the eternal. We appraise the value of this life more highly than we appraise the value of our eternal lives. It saddens me that we are willing to give up so much for so little. The trade is obscene. It is unthinkable that we choose to set eternal life aside for thrills, highs, buzzes, releases, strokes, attention, and fleeting moments of importance. Those who will be eternally lost are the descendants of Esau who exchanged his generational birthright to satisfy the immediate need of hunger. Esau is a tragic figure in scripture who traded his birthright in exchange for a bowl of stew. Anyone who sells his or her soul for this life is ten times the fool Esau was.

> **He refused to give anything less than Himself for your soul. He would not sell you short. He did not attach a dollar amount to your redemption for there is no dollar amount greater than the value of one single soul.**

We give our souls for so little. However, consider that in contrast to what Jesus was willing to give in exchange for your soul. He refused to give anything less than Himself for your soul. He would not sell you short. He did not attach a dollar amount to your redemption for there is no dollar amount greater than the value of one single soul. "Knowing that you were not redeemed with corruptible things like silver or gold, from your aimless conduct received by the tradition from your fathers, but with the precious blood of Christ, as a lamb without blemish and without spot" (1 Peter 1:18-19).

If Jesus valued your soul so highly, maybe you should too. My prayer is that you will experience an elevated sense of your worth. My hope is that you will not be willing to sell yourself short any longer. My hope is that you will desire to engage in a different trade. Instead of exchanging your soul for worldly awards, exchange your sins for Christ's righteousness. Give your imperfections in exchange for His perfection. The salvation exchange rate is much more equitable. It works out in our behalf. We give our little in exchange for Christ's greater. The exchange only seems good if you recognize that this world is passing away and that we are just pilgrims journeying through to a better place. You cannot rejoice in the exchange until you have fully committed to a city whose builder and maker is God. If we only have hope in this life, the sacrifices seem too great. But once we cross over, we will witness, along with all of the redeemed, that "Heaven was cheap enough" when we finally get home.

REFLECTION

Review (What struck you personally)?

_____
_____
_____
_____
_____

Revelation (What is God Saying to You)?

_____
_____
_____
_____
_____

Response (What are you going to do today)?

_____
_____
_____
_____
_____

11

READINESS IS RELATIONAL

Therefore, stay awake, for you do not know on what day your Lord is coming. But know this, that if the master of the house had known in what part of the night the thief was coming, he would have stayed awake and would not have let his house be broken into. Therefore you also must be ready, for the Son of Man is coming at an hour you do not expect.
Matthew 24:42-44

Heaven-bound believers are called to live in a state of watchfulness and readiness. The New Testament is filled with the constant refrain for us to watch, pray, and live soberly so that we can be ready when Jesus Christ comes. To clue us in, Jesus articulated many of the signs that would proceed His coming. In vivid detail, Jesus described the unrest that would continue to mature in the earth right up to the point when He comes. He described a world that would become progressively more violent as nation rose against nation and kingdom stood up against kingdom. He described a world that would become progressively more difficult to occupy as He predicted aggressive famine, pestilences, and catastrophes. These are "signs" that our redemption is getting closer.

Although the signs are worth our attention, please understand that knowing the signs won't save you and watching the signs won't make you ready. Readiness is relational. That might seem like a strange thing to say, but the Word validates this belief. There were signs of the coming flood in Noah's day. The first sign was the prophetic preaching of Noah which they arrogantly ignored. The antediluvians took note of animals lining up in groups and getting on the ark. They saw clouds gather in the sky, but they paid it no mind. They witnessed the remaining animals marching to high ground in anticipation of impending doom. They saw the signs, but they did not heed them.

To the person who is not in a relationship with God, signs will be perceived as coincidences, outliers, or anomalies. An unconverted person will not be reformed by "signs." They will not modify their behavior because of the "signs." An unconverted person will see the signs and perhaps repent temporarily and as soon as their fear erodes, they will go right back to their normal patterns. Others will explain the signs away through the use of science, technology, or human reason.

We are living through a season where coronavirus is not viewed as a sign, but only a passing inconvenience that will be soon treated through vaccines. The fires that raged across the western part of the United States are seen as a byproduct of global warming, an issue that can be resolved through more careful attention to the environment. The growing number of mass shootings is attributed to the rise of mental illness rather than evil. The belief is that these behaviors can be treated through therapy and access to medicine. There is a myriad of things that wave caution flags and a number of things happening in real time that cry warning like the flashing lights at a railroad crossing. Yet, we are simply moving forward while we rationalize what we see, and we push on with life as if there is no end to it.

It is my contention that readiness will never occur because of signs; readiness is the result of relationship. If you want to make Heaven your home, the most active thing you can do is deepen your relationship with Jesus. Constantly watching the signs won't make you ready; it will make you numb to the signs. This is why the first and greatest commandment is as follows,

"Jesus replied: 'Love the Lord your God with all your heart and with all your soul and with all your mind'" (Matthew 22:37).

There is a reason that the greatest and most important commandment is a call for us to love God the most. Love for God is the catalyst for readiness. Love for God is the foundation of watchfulness. Only those who are in love with Him in the present will be waiting and watching for Him at the end. Those outside of relationship will ignore and explain the signs away. Those in a relationship will see the signs and begin to daily let go of their attachments to the things of this life, making themselves ready to go home.

My seven-year-old daughter is now into texting. She is team Daddy all the way. When I'm at work during the day, she will periodically text to ask me when I am coming back home. On some days, when I am unable to give her an exact time, I have to give her an approximation. I may say, "I'll be back shortly after dark." Or I may say, "I'll be back between 7 or 8:00 pm." I may let her know that I will be back after dinner and I may give her some signs to watch for. On more than one occasion, when I pull into the cul-de-sac and enter into the driveway, my front door is already open and she is standing there waiting for me to come back even though she didn't know the exact time.

When I ask how she knew I was almost home, she'll say that she's been watching since it got dark or since 7:00 pm or since they finished eating dinner. She'll also mention that she couldn't wait for me to come back, so she kept watching. My daughter's readiness is relational. The "signs" didn't make her ready; her love for me is what made her ready. It was her love that kept her watching. The signs just helped her know how to adjust her priorities.

I desperately want to be ready when Jesus Christ comes. I don't want to be like the five foolish virgins who were sleeping when the cry of the bride and groom was made in Matthew 25. I don't want to be like the antediluvians who watched animals get on the ark while they remained outside. I don't want to be so busy making a life that I miss out on eternal life. I don't want to be so busy furnishing the house that I miss out on going to my eternal home. My focus is to build a real love relationship with Jesus.

> **Sign-watching without Savior-knowing leads to an endless stream of conspiracy theories, alarmist tendencies, and false beliefs.**

My goal is to make Jesus my obsession. It is to seek Him early and often and develop a fellowship that causes me to yearn for Heaven. I want my relationship with Him to be the foundation of my readiness. My love for Jesus will keep me watching. My love for Jesus will keep me sober. My love for Jesus will form an inexhaustible supply of readiness. The signs of the times don't create readiness; they simply confirm my faith in His word. If you know the signs, but you don't know Jesus, it is fanaticism. Sign-watching without Savior-knowing leads to an endless stream of conspiracy theories, alarmist tendencies, and false beliefs. It is critical that we pay attention to the signs, but it is most critical that we pay attention to the Savior. Readiness is relational.

REFLECTION

Review (What struck you personally)?

Revelation (What is God Saying to You)?

Response (What are you going to do today)?

12

LOOKING THROUGH A GLASS

But when that which is perfect is come, then that which is in part shall be done away...For now we see through a glass, darkly; but then face to face: now I know in part; but then shall I know even as also I am known.
1 Corinthians 13:10; 12

Innovations in technology never cease to amaze me. Just when you think boundaries can't be pushed any further, something comes along that changes the way we do life. In the last ten years, the way we communicate has radically changed. There was a time when videoconferencing was high-level technology reserved for the elite. However, innovations such as FaceTime and Zoom allow us to have face-to-face conversation via telephone or computer.

As a pastor, I have a profound appreciation for this particular innovation as once or twice a month, I am called away from home to preach or share in some type of meeting or revival.

FaceTime has become a staple in my home. With the click of a button, I can dialogue face-to-face with my wife who still does her hair and gets dressed up for our FaceTime

appointments. When I call, the kids can see me and I can see them. Talking to them on FaceTime is like watching an earthquake camera as they run and jump and do all manner of things during the conversation. It allows us to stay connected in a more personal and intimate way.
You would think that this type of personal, face-to-face interaction would make my need to see them in person less urgent. Although while using it I can see them, our home, and also share in their activities of the day, FaceTime doesn't satisfy my longing to return home. FaceTime certainly helps, but there is no substitute for seeing them all in person. No matter how much I talk to them over the course of a given trip, I am still left feeling hollow and unsatisfied. It's much better than writing a letter or sending a postcard. It's an upgrade from talking on the phone. However, it is still a limited exchange because, at the end of the day, viewing my family through my iPad is just "looking through a glass dimly."

I understand now why Paul communicated to the church with such urgency about Christ's second coming. That urgency ripened as he described the limitations of our interactions with God as "looking through a glass dimly." Those limitations will not be canceled until we get home where we will be able to see Him "face to face." Paul has clearly had very close encounters with God. In Acts 9, he experienced a direct conversation with Jesus Himself after he was knocked from his horse on the way to Damascus. Paul, by his own admission, experienced "an abundance of revelations" (2 Corinthians 12:7). He encountered God through visions, dreams, theophany, prayer, and study, yet he still viewed all of these as insufficient. The reason every mechanism for spiritual connection leaves us somewhat frustrated is because we were designed for face-to-face dialogue and in-person interaction. Don't get me wrong; prayer is essential. It is the breath of the soul. The scriptures are our nourishment and our daily sustenance.

Text messages, direct messages, FaceTime, phone calls, emails, Instagram, letters, telegrams, tweets, Tinder, and

> I've come to realize that the need for face-to-face interaction is genetic. There is a void in our genes, passed down from our first parents, that created a yearning for personal interaction with God. Because mankind was created to walk next to the Almighty, no other interaction will ever fully suffice.

Tik Tok are all limited in how much intimacy they are able to foster. In the same way, our souls will yearn for a more integrated interaction with God until the day He appears. I used to wonder why that need was so great, especially in light of the fact that I've never had face-to-face interaction with God. I've come to realize that the need for face-to-face interaction is genetic. There is a void in our genes, passed down from our first parents, that created a yearning for personal interaction with God. Because mankind was created to walk next to the Almighty, no other interaction will ever fully suffice.

Think about it. After Adam and Eve had been run out of the garden of Eden and God instructed them fully on how they were to maneuver in a sin-cursed world and after He gave them instructions on how to work the land, manage cattle, make fire, and give offerings, Heaven became silent. The gap between God and man incrementally widened the longer Adam lived. Imagine how awkward it was for Adam to kneel on the ground, drop his head in homage, and close his eyes in an attempt to pray. I can see him frustrated as his mind began to wonder as ours do in prayer. He was agitated like we are by the fact that he fell asleep during prayer. This forfeited access to God felt like a judgment too heavy for him to bear.

I can see a river of tears falling from Adam and Eve's faces as they settle into this new normal—looking dimly through a glass. Eve can handle the pain that will accompany childbirth. Adam can accept that his work will be difficult as he wrestles with thorns, briars, and thistles. The newly fallen couple can make peace with their mortality and the horrific inevitability of death. The part of the curse that they lament until the day they die is the fact that they will not be able to share in fellowship with God in the same way until the Messiah comes a second time. That personal yearning for God is genetically passed down to every generation. That void is what creates a yearning for heavenly fellowship. Because we have not been able to identify what creates that void, we try to fill it with the material trappings of this world only to find ourselves even more frustrated.

I love FaceTime; however, looking through the glass is not enough. I'm always happiest when my journey comes to an end because I look forward to taking to the skies and heading toward the place I call home. I drive down my street with anticipation and I open the front door with eagerness as I look to be reunited with those whom I love. Friends of mine, I love church, prayer, and Bible study, but it is not enough. I look forward to the day when this life journey comes to an end and the separation season is complete. When Jesus Christ comes, we also will take to the skies and head toward our heavenly home. We will walk down golden streets to the city that has the appearance of emeralds. We will enthusiastically burst through doors/gates of pearls and find our King Jesus on the other side, waiting to welcome us home. I look forward to the day when we can experience the type of fellowship we were designed to have. What a great privilege will be ours! We will be able to sit with Jesus, walk with Jesus, and talk with Jesus, never to be separated from Him again. I am reminded of the words of the great hymn that states, "Blessed assurance, Jesus is mine. Oh, what a foretaste of glory divine. Heir of salvation, purchased of God, born of His Spirit, washed in His blood. This is our story; this is our song. Praising our Savior all the day long."

This is more than theory. This is the promise that has been engineered for those who love God. This is a pilgrim promise. It is for those who are passing through—His promises for those in search of a better land. It is for those who have refused to make their greatest investments in this world. This is the promise for those who look forward to the day when they can call Heaven their home.

REFLECTION

Review (What struck you personally)?

Revelation (What is God Saying to You)?

Response (What are you going to do today)?

13

MATERIALISM

For the love of money is a root of all kinds of evil, for which some have strayed from the faith in their greediness and pierced themselves through with many sorrows.
1 Timothy 6:10

No one can serve two masters. Either you will hate the one and love the other, or you will be devoted to the one and despise the other. You cannot serve both God and money.
Matthew 6:24

This will be the most unpopular chapter in this book. It will be unpopular because it challenges us in areas where our sin is most deeply entrenched. In our western, affluent world, materialism is God's chief rival for our devotion and loyalty. Our appetite for things that sparkle, status symbols, and financial gain are greater than our appetite for God. Some of you reading might be tempted to think, "Money is no temptation because I don't really have any." The truth is that you don't have to have much money to be materialistic. Some of us have very little disposable money, but are still full of envy, covetousness, and chronic lust for things that are right outside of our price range. No matter the financial state, all must guard against the general principle of materialism.

Materialism is not unique to our age or region of the

world. Money, not idolatry, has always been the primary reason that man has abandoned God. What alienated Cain from God was his desire to keep the "fat portions" of his flock for himself. Baal worship was a distraction for Israel because it impacted the men of Israel's financial bottom line. In covenant with God, you are asked for a tenth of your income as a tithe to God along with a liberal thanks offering. The reason Baal worship was so appealing was because Baal required no such financial sacrifice. The offerings made to Baal were not self-sacrificing; instead, they were self-indulgent.

The rich young ruler was offered eternal life by Jesus and walked away sorrowful because his heart was attached to his "many possessions." Even Judas betrayed the son of God for 30 pieces of silver. In Acts chapter 5, we are introduced to a couple, Ananias and Saphira, who were struck down by the Holy Spirit because they placed money ahead of mission and the commitment they had made to God. The apostle Paul even warned Timothy to guard himself against the love of money, the foundation of all evil. He warned that greed was the reason "some have strayed from the faith in their greediness, and pierced themselves through with many sorrows" (1 Timothy 6:10).

Throughout salvation history, mankind has consistently said "No" to Heaven in exchange for material possessions. Materialism is the primary threat to the spiritual well-being of God's last day, Laodicean church, which is described as "rich and increased with goods, having need of nothing." Jesus was intentional in describing money as God's chief antithesis or rival for the human heart. Very clearly, He stated that no man can serve two masters. It is impossible for us to show equal allegiance to more than one ruler because we would "love one and hate the other." Jesus' statement of impossibility is clear. The God that created us says that it is impossible for us to love money and/or materialism while fully loving Him at the same time. Love for one of those will directly result in neglect or hate for the other. It seems hyperbolic to say that man will actually hate the other.

That statement used to challenge me. As a younger believer, it just didn't resonate. I thought that I could love God and still have some room to love other things and possessions. The reason I held to this faulty belief is that I didn't quite understand how love worked. The funny thing about love is that it operates in an imbalanced way. Love's attention is focused and concentrated. Love cannot be diluted, and its loyalty cannot be split. Love is so potently aimed in a singular direction that it shows up in the form of hate toward everything that is a rival to the object of its affection.

Love for "this" shows up as neglect for "that." To show love in one location requires it to be withdrawn from another location. Case in point: as a young man, I loved to hang out with my friends. I had a group of guys that I am still very tight with. We played ball, watched sports, and did guy things together. However, when I began to fall in love with Gianna and started to consider marrying her, I didn't realize it, but my entire energy shifted. I was still cool with my friends, but the bulk of my time was focused on Gianna. I gave her my attention and my devotion was aimed in her direction. My love for her showed up in the form of neglect in some of my other relationships. Any attention shown my other female friends evaporated and my time with the guys was cut down to a minimum. My love for her created an unintended neglect toward my previous loyalties.

When Gianna and I looked to buy our first home, we viewed dozens of houses in our search. We scoured the multiple listing system in search of our starter home. However, when we looked at one particular model in Georgetown, Kentucky, we instantly fell in love. Our hearts instantly attached to it and we put down earnest money that same day. Our love for that house caused us to stop searching. We didn't need to see anything else. I never viewed another house after that because when you discover something that you love, you won't need to look at anything else beyond it. In the same way, from a spiritual perspective, love for materialism can be so strong and so powerful that it can begin to slowly nullify your relationship with God. You can so fully devote or attach yourself to things that you stop searching for God who is greater than things. Time spent seeking God will be reduced to a minimum because you are so devoted to your pursuit of possessions.

We would all agree that a man cannot be equally devoted to two wives. You can't be devoted to the Lakers and the Celtics. You can't be devoted to the Yankees and the Red Sox. You can't be truly devoted to the Redskins and the Cowboys. Devotion to one makes you instantly at odds with its rival.

> **Money doesn't just try to rival God; it seeks to replace God in our lives.**

The reason that money has such a strong hold over humanity is that it pledges to do and be what only God can do and be for us. Money masquerades as happiness. For many of us, money equals security. Too often we equate money with importance. Frequently, our very sense of worth is connected to what we have or where we live. Money doesn't just try to rival God; it seeks to replace God in our lives. The Word says that many will depart from the faith because they are chasing a financial illusion, only to be pierced with many challenges.

The piercing comes from the extreme disappointment of misplaced expectations and foolish pursuits. At some point, circumstances of life reveal the limitations of money and will pierce with such painful pricks that it will cause money's limitations to become obvious. When the weight of life is bearing down on your soul, it becomes obvious what money can't buy. Money can't buy a good night's sleep. Money can't buy inner peace. Money can't make you secure about who you are. There is no brand of clothing that can cover the holes in your soul. All of the money in the world can't get you into the Kingdom of Heaven. When it comes down to salvation, there is only one type of currency that is accepted. We can only be redeemed from sin through the "shedding of blood" (Hebrews 9:22). True value is not derived by what you have. In order to discern your value, don't look at your bank account. Instead, look at your price tag. It is not the wages that you are paid that makes you valuable; it is the price that was paid for your redemption that validates your significance. Just a point of clarity. Money is not evil, nor is having nice things immoral. The issue comes when we attach too much significance to material things. The sin is our devotion to materialism. It is when the pursuit of things controls are movements, decisions, and priorities. God has an interesting way of showing us how unimportant possessions truly are. First, when He appears at His second coming, He will burn every possession that was stitched, built, mined, or manufactured. No earthly possession will make the journey to Heaven. When you read John's description of Heaven's New Jerusalem in Revelation 21, you will notice that the streets are made of gold, the gates are made of pearls, and the twelve foundations are made of twelve, precious stones.

From our earthly vantage point, it looks as if God is espousing opulence. The exact opposite is true. The golden streets in Heaven reveal that gold has the same value as asphalt here on earth. Gates made of pearls show that, in Heaven, pearls are tantamount to the value of the wood or iron we use to make our gates. The twelve stones that make up the twelve foundations contain value equivalent to concrete. He devalues what we deem precious by treating it as builders grade material in heaven. Even the golden crowns that will be given to us will be cast down at the Savior's feet because they will have no value to us in light of all that God has accomplished on our behalf.

If those things have no value in eternity, why should we seek and sacrifice for them so much here on earth? Instead of us living lives driven by materialistic values, let us live seeking a different set of goods. Let's pursue peace. Let's seek simplicity. Let's make contact with Christ our goal. Let's attach greater value to love and meaningful relationships. Let's estimate wisdom more highly. Let's not focus on things that adorn a home. Instead, let's set our primary focus on going home.

REFLECTION

Review (What struck you personally)?

_____
_____
_____
_____
_____

Revelation (What is God Saying to You)?

_____
_____
_____
_____
_____

Response (What are you going to do today)?

_____
_____
_____
_____
_____

14

SOUL TIES

Do not be misled: Bad company corrupts good character.
1 Corinthians 15:33

When I was in school, I once heard someone say that if you show me your friends, I'll show you your future. That statement may not be 100% accurate, but it is loaded with truth. That person was speaking of the power of partnership. Who you partner with or tie your soul to can determine so many of your outcomes. Great partnerships can push you beyond your perceived potential. I noticed something about feeble attempts to get in shape. There are a certain number of push-ups that I think I can do when I'm by myself. However, if I am with someone who exercises frequently and I am being pushed, that accountability nudges me further than I would normally go by myself. When I'm jogging alone, one mile takes me a certain amount of time to cover. When jogging with others, I tend to move faster than my normal pace. Good partnerships can bring out the best in you. On the other hand, poor partnerships can harm your goals as well as objectives. Try attempting to eat healthy if you go to lunch every day with people who are dessert fiends or if you work in an office where pastries are frequently present. You may stand your ground for some time, but eventually the influence of the group will begin to wear you down.

I learned the importance of selecting good partnerships in middle school. My science teacher allowed us to do our science projects in groups. She permitted us to choose our own partners. Looking back, I realize that this was not just an exercise in science, it was designed to teach us some essential, social lessons as well. I didn't realize that my grade, in many ways, would be determined even before I started working. My grade would be decided by the individuals with whom I chose to partner. The teacher would not parse out our solo effort and grade us on how we individually performed. Instead, we would all get the same grade no matter how well or how poorly we individually performed. The strength of the partnership or lack thereof determined my grade.

I made the mistake of partnering with a couple of the guys that were on my basketball team. We were buddies and I chose fun over functionality. I realized that this was going to be a catastrophe while not far into the project. They were not as concerned with their final grade as I was. They were content to let me do the heavy lifting while they just came along for the ride. The workload assigned was of such a nature that no one person could carry the group. Every member would have to do his part in order for the group to thrive. Even though my work was competent on this project, our group grade was still a C- because poor partnership sabotaged my best efforts.

{ **Great partnerships push, but poor partnerships paralyze.** }

Great partnerships push, but poor partnerships paralyze. Over the course of your life, your happiness, success, and eternal results will reflect how wisely or how poorly you choose your partnerships. We must be very prayerful about who we partner with in friendships, business, and especially in romance as we seek to head home. The soul ties that bind your heart to another's have the ability to push you toward the Kingdom of Heaven. Those same romantic, soul ties can fasten you to this world that is destined to burn. The Bible is replete with admonitions to choose your company carefully. "He who walks with the wise will become wise, but the companion of fools will be destroyed" (Proverbs 13:20). "Do not be misled: Bad company corrupts good character." (1 Corinthians 15:33). None of us walks through life unaffected by our environment or our partnerships. Don't overestimate your strength. We can all be influenced, moved, or swayed from principal and correct practice.

If you are contemplating marriage, the consideration you should give the most weight to is your potential partner's spirituality. Will he or she be the wind in the sails of your life that pushes you toward your destinations or will he or she be an anchor that hinders your forward motion. Although looks matter, they will ultimately fade. Income is important, but it is not the most important thing. How cute you look together in a picture is a vain and foolish consideration.

> **Once you fasten yourself to him or her emotionally, sexually, and spiritually, the merger, in many ways, guarantees that wherever he or she ends up will also be where you end up.**

Instead, evaluate whether or not that person loves God. Does he or she lead a Christ-centered life? Is Heaven his or her ultimate goal? Once you fasten yourself to him or her emotionally, sexually, and spiritually, the merger, in many ways, guarantees that wherever he or she ends up will also be where you end up. When making this choice, decide with your head and not only your heart. Choose according to the Spirit rather than your lust. No earthly relationship is worth sacrificing your heavenly tie to Jesus Christ and your eternal home.

The same is true in friendship. As you march through this life, you need people in your inner circle who know how to get a prayer through. When life is hard, you need people who will speak life rather than death. In seasons of confusion, you need counsel that is Godly not carnal. You need friends that think faith, talk faith and live faith. Good friends don't just want something when you have it; they want you when you have nothing. Good friends don't just stand next to you when you are down; they cheer for you when you are on the assent. They celebrate your victories as if they are theirs and they never put their jealousies above your happiness.

Jesus knew the importance of partnership. It is why He sent the disciples out in groups of two: Moses had Aaron, Elijah had Elisha, Joshua had Caleb, and Paul had Silas. Naomi had Ruth and Mary had Elizabeth. In scripture, you don't see any great men or great woman standing alone. Instead, they are supported by people assigned to help them live out the calling that God had for them. Wherever you see greatness, there is great partnership. Wherever you see failure, there is poor partnership. Adam did not rebuke Eve; he partnered with her in transgression. Samson became ensnared through sexual partnership with Delilah. Ahab was overwhelmed by the strong influence of Jezebel. And the wisest man to ever live—Solomon—married ungodly wives who caused his heart to be turned away from God.

The work for someone today is to start detaching from some partnerships. Someone needs to begin by decluttering your heart by severing toxic soul ties. The work for somebody tonight is to have an awkward conversation with a boyfriend or girlfriend. Another's need is to unfriend, unfollow, or close down your Tinder account. Someone needs to dissolve some partnerships and look for support in the body of Christ instead of in the nightclub or local tavern. There is too much at stake. Heaven is on the line. Eternal life is up for grabs. You're rolling the dice with eternity. Don't leave it up to chance. If you show me your friends, I can show you your future. Choose well.

REFLECTION

Review (What struck you personally)?

_____
_____
_____
_____

Revelation (What is God Saying to You)?

_____
_____
_____
_____

Response (What are you going to do today)?

_____
_____
_____
_____

15

REAPPROPRIATING VALUE

If someone else thinks they have reasons to put confidence in the flesh, I have more: circumcised on the eighth day, of the people of Israel, of the tribe of Benjamin, a Hebrew of Hebrews; in regard to the law, a Pharisee; as for zeal, persecuting the church; as for righteousness based on the law, faultless. But whatever were gains to me I now consider loss for the sake of Christ. What is more, I consider everything a loss because of the surpassing worth of knowing Christ Jesus my Lord, for whose sake I have lost all things. I consider them garbage, that I may gain Christ and be found in him, not having a righteousness of my own that comes from the law, but that which is through faith in Christ—the righteousness that comes from God on the basis of faith. I want to know Christ—yes, to know the power of his resurrection and participation in his sufferings, becoming like him in his death, and so, somehow, attaining to the resurrection from the dead.
Philippians 3:4-11

I once had the opportunity to conduct pre-marital counseling with a wonderful, young couple in their late twenties. There are times when I walk with certain couples through this process with trepidation because it is clear they should get as far away from each other as they possibly can. However, with this couple, there was no such anxiety. Their love for each other came out in their speech as well as their body language and even seemed to ooze from their pores. They were mature and spiritual. They had a uniquely accurate grasp of what they were getting into. The counseling was going uncomfortably smooth as it seemed to be too good to be true. Then it happened.

One afternoon, I was scheduled to meet with both of them when the groom-to-be showed up alone. He stated that he wanted to talk to me alone before his fiancé came, which made my stomach sink. He had an uneasiness and an anxiety about him that I had never witnessed. He stated that he had been keeping some news from his fiancé for about two days and was nervous to share it with her. He wanted to break the news to her in counseling that day. The way he set this scenario up made me want to run and hide.

The happy couple had been planning to begin their life together here in Huntsville. Two days prior to our counseling appointment, he had found out that his job would be transferring him to another state where opportunities for her line of work would be hard to come by. She had a financially lucrative job here in the city. She quickly scaled the ranks and had been promoted three times in the last two years due to her discipline and work ethic. She loved what she did and had major career earnings to prove it. He was ambivalent about how to bring it up. He stated that he wanted some advice on how to share it when the truth was, he wanted to make me an accomplice in his ambush by using me to help buffer her reaction.

We talked through a number of scenarios that included going, staying, and commuting. We committed the matter to prayer and awaited her arrival. I was a little anxious for them because this was a big thing he was asking her to walk away from. She had built equity in her job, she had sacrificed for it, and she was important there. I remember the look of surprise on her face when she walked in and saw him seated already. After we prayed,

I communicated that her fiancé told me that he had been keeping some news from her that would potentially impact their marriage.

Tears began to form in her eyes, but she was just composed enough that they did not fall. She began to grip the armrest of her chair as a thousand different scenarios raced through her head. You could see her emotionally bracing herself for unanticipated bad news. He detailed what happened with his job, where they would have to live, and the lack of opportunities for her. He then began to brace himself for the fallout of her reaction.

This heavy build-up was suddenly deflated by her surprise reaction. She exhaled with relief as she calmly stated, "Is that all?" We were both surprised by her lack of reaction. The bride-to-be expressed her love for the groom-to-be. She told him that commuting between states was not an option for her. She almost immediately began to make plans to let her job know that after the wedding, she would have to resign. I am a big believer in family over finances, but I wanted to make sure that she had thought it through and that she was not making too hasty a decision. Her mind was made up. After the wedding, they would leave as a family and start their life together.

> **But her love for him, made that job of zero importance.**
>
> **When the job stood at variance with her true love, it never stood a chance.**

I was not totally surprised at her decision. I have seen both brides and grooms-to-be make these types of choices. What surprised me was that she gave it little to no thought. What shocked me was that commuting or losing him was not even a consideration. She had a valuable job and she contributed much to that job. Up to this point in her life, this job was the most important thing she had going. But her love for him, made that job of zero importance. Her desire to be with her groom caused her to reappropriate the value that had been attached to this job. When the job stood at variance with her true love, it never stood a chance.

This experience reminded me of the words penned to the Philippian church by the apostle Paul. He talked in great detail about how he reappropriated the things that once held value to him before Christ. There were numerous metrics that he had once used to qualify his importance. He was circumcised on the eighth day according to Jewish law, which gave him spiritual significance. He was a member of the tribe of Benjamin, which gave him cultural significance. He was a flawless Pharisee, which gave him career significance and a "Hebrew of Hebrews," which gave him social significance. His religion, his cultural distinction along with his work and social standings were the constructs that gave him identity, value, significance, and worth. He was set apart by the day of his circumcision. He was proud of his cultural and ethnic identity. He basked in his elevated career station, and he reveled in the social admiration that all of these things brought his way. Paul was important.

> "I consider them garbage, that I may gain Christ and be found in him"

However, like the bride-to-be, when those things which once brought significance were set in contrast with his true love, there was nothing left to consider. Paul's love for Jesus was so strong that it nullified the importance these things once had. He uses the strongest possible language to describe the value of all earthly constructs that seek to attach themselves to our hearts. He says, "I consider them garbage, that I may gain Christ and be found in him" (Philippians 3:8). His love for Christ required a radical reappropriating of values for the believer. Notice that Paul does not renounce these things. He was saying that the value they brought him had changed. What changed their value? What caused them to be valued on the same level as trash was Paul's desire to "be found in Him." The desire to "attain the resurrection of the dead" made this life and all of its tributes and trappings worthless. It was his desire to go home to be fully united with Christ that caused him to re-evaluate what he attached value to.

What are the things that you are attaching too much value to? What earthly construct is propping you up? What is competing with God for your affections? What is bringing you so much value that it rivals the love of Jesus for first place in your life? Is it work? Is it money? Is it your big screen television or video games? Is it your wardrobe? Is it your title? Is it a relationship? What makes you consider this world home or while you classify Heaven as your Air B&B, the home you may or may not visit.

Today's call is not for you to renounce anything. It's not asking you to quit a job, burn a wardrobe, disown friends or smash your vehicle. I'm asking you to evaluate how much value you have attached to these things. My contention is that we are not ready to go home until we can say with truth like Paul that "I count it all as garbage." The important part is not the what; it's the why—that we "might be found in Him." The why is so that "we might know Him and the power of His resurrection. The why is so that when this life is over and our work on earth is done, we can "attain the resurrection of the dead." Like the previously mentioned bride-to-be, the decision is that simple. There is not anything to really consider. When weighing these things, our desire to go home must easily outweigh everything else.

Made in the USA
Middletown, DE
03 May 2025

75050356R00056